Starting Practice

THE ESSENTIAL HANDBOOK

COLLEEN SULLIVAN &
GEOFFREY MEREDITH

National Library of Australia cataloguing-in-publication entry:

Starting practice: The essential handbook

Authors: Sullivan, Colleen and Meredith, Geoffrey.

1. Practice management

2. Healthcare practice.

3. Healthcare practitioner support.

Editor: Ellie Gleeson www.lemotjuste.com.au

Book design and typesetting by BookCoverCafe.com

ISBN:
978-0-9942263-0-3 (pbk)
978-0-9942263-1-0 (ebk)

Acknowledgment

We acknowledge our families who have always inspired, encouraged, and supported each of us.

We also acknowledge our friends and colleagues in healthcare who are so happy to share their knowledge and experiences.

In particular, we would like to thank our editor, Ellie Gleeson, who has worked patiently and expertly with us to bring our second book to publication.

Dedication

We dedicate this book to those medical practitioners, dental practitioners, physiotherapists, and other healthcare providers who have decided to enter private practice.

Table of Contents

Foreword

Ms Colleen Sullivan and Professor Geoffrey Meredith have once again combined their talents to produce the must-have handbook on starting practice. This work, in the tradition of some recent great authors, is the "prequel" to their last, very successful, book *Successful Practice Management: Exceeding Patient Expectations*. This book provides a guide to the foundation and framework within a professional practice that assists the delivery of goals in their original work of "exceeding patient expectations".

Once again we find the guidance is clearly set out to help clinicians, practice managers, and staff avoid making those common mistakes that can really set back a new business. Sullivan and Meredith effectively combine their 60 years of experience in an easy to read practical guide.

Preparation and planning are covered, as well as potential business structures that should be considered. The role and use of information technology to grow efficiency and maximise financial performance is there and so is a chapter on the importance of training and maintaining high-quality staff.

Once the basics are in place, we find a chapter on networking and promotion to attract and retain quality patients in an environment that will deliver both patient and staff satisfaction.

If you are looking to reduce your business risk then start right here.

Dr. Steve Hambleton
Specialist General Practitioner
Immediate Past President of the Australian Medical Association

Preface

In Australia, we have a large number of healthcare practitioners who work in either the public health system and or in private practice. Many of these practitioners make the decision to enter private practice. For many, this decision can be daunting. However, it should also be seen as an opportunity to deliver quality healthcare to patients in an environment that is happy, supportive, and successful for all involved.

This book addresses:
- how to start your healthcare career in private practice
- how to establish and run a practice
- how to join an existing practice
- what is involved operating a successful private practice.

Professional healthcare practices are complex organisations. Each practice reflects the specific interests, attitudes, and aspirations of individual professionals who are responsible for decisions that relate to the operating and establishment of the practice.

A practice involves a myriad of issues, ranging from organisational formats, practice business operations, use of technology, management, staffing options, patient needs, risk and compliance, services offered, finance options, work-life balance, planning for future sustainability and development—any of these issues, plus more, are a feature of any one practice.

It is impossible for one book to explore all the issues that relate to running a practice and working in a practice. However, the 11 chapters in this book identify a range of options available to a healthcare professional interested in establishing or joining a practice. We provide a host of information and suggestions so that the individual can determine their own preferences for practice establishment/employment. We present you with options to allow you to make your own decisions as to what best meets your needs at this point in your career—whether you are a graduate or an established professional.

To assist in this, at the end of each chapter we have written a checklist which is a series of questions that prompt you to focus on certain topics and provide answers to specific questions. Your answers to these will assist you in making the right choices.

Each chapter highlights the key factors which may be included in any decision regarding employment in an existing practice or establishing a new practice. At no point do we attempt to nominate any ONE set of options—rather, we provide suggestions, guidance, and advice as to what, in our experience, are the recommendations for action to achieve a successful practice and, in turn, a successful career for you.

We encourage flexibility in practice design and structure and recognise that individual attitudes are critical in any practice success.

This book is a response to the comments and requests by so many healthcare practitioners who have spoken to us over many years. They all talk about wishing they had the knowledge and understanding of all the issues involved in starting a practice. These practitioners had spent many years studying then working in the healthcare system and were about to enter the next phase of their careers in entering private practice.

This book sets out to provide anyone starting a practice with the information, ideas, and tools to make the most of this opportunity.

Chapter 1: The Qualities to Establish a Successful Healthcare Practice

Why was this book written?

New enterprises or businesses, whether they are professional practices or commercial ventures, are seen as significant for any community. These new enterprises help drive communities forward and have a positive flow-on effect on the national economy. It follows that those who wish to establish new enterprises (often referred to as entrepreneurs) are to be encouraged and supported.

Statistics[1] show that approximately 20 percent or more of the workforce are self-employed. This proportion of the population is a significant driving force for the community. The self-employed workforce needs to be recognised and assisted as they are critical suppliers of competition in the marketplace and provide unique services that meet the specialised needs of various consumer groups, including patients of healthcare practices.

Having said this, we have to acknowledge that establishing any kind of new enterprise (be it a professional practice or

---

1   See the Australian Bureau of Statistics: www.abs.gov.au.

commercial enterprise) represents a risk. Thousands of would-be self-employers fail in their business attempts within the initial 12 months of operation and this comes at a high cost to themselves, their partners and families, and to the community in general.

There are three main purposes of this book:

1. to encourage and support those interested in establishing an independent professional practice in healthcare to be successful and profitable
2. to encourage and support those starting into an independent professional practice either as a partner, an associate, or an employed practitioner to make that practice a successful enterprise
3. to provide a series of practical guidelines and recommendations for the establishment of a successful and profitable healthcare practice.

The 11 chapters in our book are designed to encourage self-employment in the healthcare profession and provide practical, relevant, and industry-standard advice to ensure that this self-employment is a success.

This chapter consists of 11 subsections. We begin by discussing the purpose of this book and its primary target audience before investigating the qualities of a healthcare professional that are essential for establishing a healthcare practice. This chapter concludes with a checklist to review the factors influencing self-employment.

The 11 subsections of this chapter include:

1. Why was this book written?
2. Who should read this book?
3. What topics will this book cover?
4. Qualities of a healthcare professional
5. What does it mean to be self-employed?

6. What are the personal characteristics of a healthcare practice owner?
7. Can any of these personal characteristics be developed?
8. Attitudes to work and the workplace
9. Attitudes to compliance, risk management, and workplace operations
10. Reasons not to seek self-employment in the healthcare industry
11. Checklist: Factors influencing self-employment.

Who should read this book?

Each year, thousands of individuals complete their study, work, or experience requirements to meet the professional standards required for entry into the healthcare profession. The majority of these graduates initially begin their employment in professional practices, government departments, hospitals, or other healthcare institutions. While many graduates may consider entering an independent private practice, most approach the positions of employment mentioned above as an initial step. Teaching institutions generally fail to encourage or provide information for graduates planning to enter private practice immediately upon graduation.

The list of healthcare graduates who may decide to enter independent private practice is extensive and could include:

• Medical doctors: having completed years of tertiary study, including practical experience in hospitals, opportunities exist for doctors to establish their own independent practice. These practices are highly regarded in terms of professional competence and experience.

• Dentists: similar to medical doctors, dentists complete extensive tertiary study and practical experience in dentistry hospitals or general healthcare institutions. A majority of dentists practise in an independent private practice attracting patients on a fee basis or are employed by a government department providing dentistry services for schools and the public.

This list is by no means exhaustive: of course, there are other healthcare practitioners who may consider independent practice, including audiologists, optometrists, psychologists, chiropractors, dieticians, nurses, occupational therapists, physiotherapists, podiatrists, speech pathologists, midwives, naturopaths, or veterinarians. Every major city and significant regional town has representatives of these healthcare professionals in independent private practice as well as many being employed in hospitals, government departments, or private firms.

What topics will this book cover?

This chapter examines the qualities and attitudes required by those individuals who are considering setting up an independent healthcare practice. We ask the questions to determine whether you, as a healthcare professional, have the qualities to establish your own successful private practice. The remaining 10 chapters examine the more specific aspects of these qualities and discuss precisely what is required of individuals who move into independent private practice.

Chapter Two reviews various employment options for graduates in the healthcare profession and addresses questions such as:

- Will you seek self-employment?
- Will you join a group of professionals either already in private practice or intending to enter private practice?

We examine the benefits and risks associated with these options.

Chapter Three examines the importance of patients: those in independent practice must attract and also retain patients. This chapter examines the possibility of converting patients into "practice ambassadors": patients who actively support the practice and encourage other potential patients to attend the practice.

Chapter Four examines patient satisfaction. Patient satisfaction is written about and often discussed in the healthcare industry. Currently, understanding patient needs through patient surveys is even included in practice accreditation. In this chapter, we identify some of the main barriers to patient satisfaction in the consultation process. We explore patient satisfaction at all stages of the patient's interaction with a practice and include a checklist to help maximise patient satisfaction.

Chapter Five examines a practice's "most important asset": employed staff who are trained and qualified to provide quality services to patients. This chapter acknowledges that most of the time that patients spend in an independent healthcare practice is with staff rather than with a professional as principal; therefore, staff are critical to practice success. The role of the practice manager is essential to the success of your practice. All areas of the practice need to be managed and it is important to have a person in this position with key responsibilities.

Chapter Six examines how the use of technology has allowed practices to more effectively assist and support patients and staff. The rapid pace of change in technology from year to year means that anyone interested in independent practice must be abreast of technological advances and be prepared to implement these advances into their practice.

Chapter Seven discusses issues relating to finance performance. Financial management is essential for any successful practice and those entering practice must be prepared to understand all financial aspects associated with establishing, operating, and producing profit for a practice.

Chapter Eight discusses the aspects associated with financial planning in private practice. A successful independent practice has to be financially viable to support staff, provide you as the practitioner with a salary, and to meet operating costs associated with providing healthcare services to your patients. The chapter addresses questions such as:

- Do you have an understanding of these costs?
- Do you have plans in place to maintain and monitor financial performance?

Chapter Nine analyses the issue of compliance: an essential area for the self-employed and one which is increasing in importance each year. This chapter addresses how to comply with government requirements, the requirements of various healthcare industry bodies, the requirements of health regulators, and requirements of the community. The Australian Government has taken an intense interest in independent healthcare practices and has established guidelines and rules which must be met.

Chapter Ten examines the issue of networking and promotion for practice development. It looks to the future of your practice and provides a range of plans that are designed to ensure that the practice has a stable future. These plans are formulated to maintain professional practice standards through the national system of accreditation.

Chapter Eleven provides a review of the book and gives readers the opportunity to write their own personal recommendations and areas to address based on the issues discussed in this book.

Checklists: At the end of each chapter are a series of checklists designed to assist you in practically implementing the advice and recommendations from each chapter into your practice.

Qualities of a healthcare professional

It is important to discuss the personal and professional qualities of a healthcare professional—both employed and in independent practice. The most fundamental quality of a healthcare professional is their dedication to providing support for individuals—they are "people persons". They provide care for individuals from the point of view of overall health and well-being. Healthcare professionals are dedicated, determined, optimistic, impartial, patient, and tend to be leaders. They have the ability to assess patient needs, apply professional skills in solving healthcare problems, and at the same time remain independent—all with the view to solving and improving a patient's health outcomes and lifestyle.

Healthcare professionals need to possess a high degree of interpersonal communication skills: they require patience, the ability and willingness to listen, the capacity to seek solutions to complex problems, and the ability to act as counsellors and advisors to their patients. These characteristics and qualities can produce significant rewards but can be demanding.

What does it mean to be self-employed?

In brief, it means that you are on your own—all the decisions are yours (together with the principals in your practice if you follow that option). Most likely, you will have support from dedicated and trained staff who are knowledgeable in healthcare practice matters or you might have an advisory board—a group of professionals to advise you on matters associated with your professional practice although they have no power or responsibility. Basically, every decision to be made is your decision!

In reality, what does this mean for you in terms of operating a new healthcare practice? It means making decisions on:

- Location of your practice: Where will your practice be located? Will it be as a stand-alone building or will it be included in a building that is already established? Will you own a building? Will you own an office or rent an office?

- The layout of your practice: Now that you have established the location of your practice, the question of layout has to be determined and although there are professionals who can assist, the final decisions rest with you—furnishings, furniture, paintings, colour, perhaps the introduction of sound and related issues connected with layout and presentation.

- Operating systems: This aspect of your practice is crucial to the daily functioning and operation of your practice. Document management, record keeping systems, and the practice-wide use of technology are all vital aspects that need to be established correctly from the outset. Again, there are professionals who can assist you with the implementation of these systems but the final decision as to what systems will be introduced and maintained is up to you.

- Staff: The hiring, training, and development of staff is your most important asset. It is useful to consider identifying one staff member as a practice manager and other staff members with specialist roles, such as systems operations, patient liaison, practice promotion, and record keeping.

- Workplace health and safety: Questions of occupational health and safety and management of issues related to this is an important part of your practice. As the practice principal, you are responsible for ensuring that these issues are adequately addressed.

- Practice development: Practice development, promotions, and marketing are an important aspect to your practice, particularly in ensuring the future stability and success of the practice. In what direction do you see the practice heading? What do you need to do to assist the practice to get to that point? Decisions relating to this and the means whereby you plan for the future remain with you as the self-employed owner.
- Expert advice: It is important to seek the best expert advice and recommendations—for example, on financial, legal, and marketing issues—to ensure any decisions made are done when you are fully informed. This is discussed further when we talk about a Board of Advice.
- Practice image: A task that many practice owners find difficult is to develop an image of the practice to ensure that the character and atmosphere represents your aims and objectives in creating an environment which is attractive to patients and staff.

These are major tasks for any practice owner which, if implemented correctly, can prove to be rewarding. Potential practice owners need to be aware of what is required in setting up a new healthcare practice.

What are the personal characteristics of a healthcare practice owner?

It is important to identify and discuss the personal characteristics of professionals who decide to set up their own healthcare practice. One of the most obvious characteristics is the personal drive and confidence that they can cope with the workload involved in the exercise. The characteristics related to attitudes to work and attitudes to meeting requirements of being in professional practice cannot be ignored. These are discussed below.

Discussing personal characteristics can be a sensitive issue for professionals. By accepting that certain personal characteristics are important for the self-employed, we are acknowledging that there are some individuals that should not consider self-employment. This is not a question of the level of an individual's professional knowledge or understanding but rather their personal views and attitudes which may indicate that the option of self-employment is not suitable for them and that they should continue with employment in hospitals, corporations, government departments, or established practices. Our purpose in this section is to highlight that to be self-employed in the healthcare industry requires certain personal characteristics; we recognise that certain individuals do not possess these characteristics.

The following list identifies the personal characteristics required for a healthcare practice owner:

- *Communication and willingness to listen*: Communication at all levels is an important characteristic. It involves not only the ability to give information but to get information through the ability and willingness to listen to others. This can be with patients and their families, with colleagues, and with all staff. How you communicate—whether it is through the spoken word or body language—can have a major influence on outcomes.

- *Self-confidence, self-reliance, and a positive self-image*: Self-employed professionals will come into contact with a wide variety of members of the community who have different attitudes and approaches to healthcare professionals and to their treatment options. A positive self-image is necessary to deal with such a variety of attitudes and, at times, criticism. A professional who may not wish to deal with such a wide group from the community on a daily basis is not to be criticised, but it is important to accept the importance of this attitude.

- *Willingness to accept challenges*: A practice owner faces many challengers aside from the healthcare problems he or she faces in a professional context. The challenges range from dealing with difficult members of the community (who are argumentative, belligerent, doubtful, etcetera) to tolerating and listening to a wide range of attitudes. A sense of humour in these times can be useful! Empathy, understanding, and a patient attitude are key personal characteristics of the self-employed professional.
- *Determination and commitment*: Owning and operating a practice is a full-time occupation that follows you home at night after you have closed the practice doors for the day. Having a strong sense of commitment to the practice and its success—and by extension, to associated work tasks and serving patients—are essential personal characteristics. This is coupled with a willingness and ability to listen, to communicate, and to accept many challenges posed by patients with a variety of personal, physical, and mental problems to be solved.
- *Goal-driven*: Self-employed professionals have specific goals and expectations and strive to achieve these despite the difficulties faced in operating a practice. The ability to identify, set, and work consistently towards a goal is a characteristic necessary to establish and maintain a successful, profitable practice.
- *Up-to-date*: Having completed rigorous training, it is assumed that the self-employed professional is mentally alert, knowledgeable, and committed to continuing their education by seeking out research, industry standards, and the latest clinical techniques available to the professional in his or her particular field.

The above list of personal characteristics is not exhaustive and might appear rather demanding. This is to be expected since the self-employed healthcare specialist is an important position in the community and must be taken seriously. Underpinning all of these personal characteristics is the importance of the ability to develop a practice culture and have a set of values for the whole practice.

Can any of these personal characteristics be developed?

The short answer to this question is "Yes". A starting point in this exercise is for you to consider your personal strengths and weaknesses. Don't spend a great deal of time on weaknesses but focus on your strengths. Look through the list of personal characteristics identified above and decide which of these are your major strengths.

Communication can be developed—there are key methods of communicating and, as a self-employed professional, you should be aware of these. The personal characteristics of self-confidence, self-reliance, and a positive self-image are often affected by personal appearance—this is something which you can review and take action on in a positive way. The willingness to accept challenges, displaying a sense of determination and commitment, being goal-driven, and remaining up-to-date in professional education are important and you should think about each of these and decide whether they represent strengths or weaknesses from your point of view. If they represent a weakness, then make it a priority to address these issues in your daily professional life.

As we have discussed, personal characteristics can be developed or influenced by many things including the people we work with, the environment we work in, and the situations we might face. What is important is to be aware of the characteristics that can make you a better practitioner.

Attitudes to work and the workplace

Whether you are self-employed, employed by the government, working in a private or public hospital, or private enterprise your attitude to work and the workplace are important. For the self-employed practice owner, your attitude to the workplace is critical to practice success. Some of the personal characteristics discussed above are important for attitudes to workplace—particularly the ability to communicate, self-confidence and self-reliance, and the ability and willingness to listen. In addition, the following considerations are important when discussing attitudes to work for the self-employed:

- Working with people in a positive manner is critical to the success of the practice.
- As the owner of a professional practice, you are expected to be a leader, providing leadership to staff and to patients.
- As a leader, you are ultimately responsible for all your actions. Be prepared to acknowledge this without any hesitation.
- It is imperative—for the image of your practice and the morale of your staff—that you demonstrate satisfaction with your employment and pride in what you have accomplished. It is important for your staff to recognise that the practice is a success and they have an important role to play in that success (this is discussed in more detail in Chapter 3).
- Focus on the future of the practice, its development, and success. This may involve the recruitment of additional professional healthcare employees to address the needs of a growing number of patients.
- Attracting and keeping patients is critical to your leadership expectations and success.
- You need to be highly-organised, professionally manage and operate your practice, spend time and resources

developing and training staff, and have the ability to address administrative problems.

- You need to recognise and foster the importance of managing staff appropriately. The use of a practice manager is critical to achieve this.

Attitudes to compliance, risk management, and workplace operations

Every healthcare practice has to address the need to comply with regulations and requirements of various organisations including government, regulatory bodies, and professional associations. While these may seem tedious or constraining, each regulation and requirement has been introduced to protect the public and provide guidance for the industry.

The compliance requirements for a practice owner may arise from:

- legislation at state or Commonwealth level
- regulatory and licensing bodies
- professional associations
- industry groups
- practice policies and procedures.

Compliance requirements must be integrated into the operations of the healthcare practice—they cannot be avoided. Compliance affects many facets of the practice. In the content below, we address the impact of compliance on the following:

- practice type and business structure
- activities and requirements of principals
- requirements of healthcare personnel other than principals
- compliance associated with services offered by the healthcare practice

- compliance associated with risk management
- compliance associated with insurance
- the management of information technology
- compliance associated with corporate governance.

Practice structure

Government policy has a major impact on the business structure of practices in the healthcare industry. The most relevant policy is taxation. All healthcare practices have to comply with taxation requirements. This means, among other requirements, that financial records must be meticulously kept as they may be open to inspection at any time by taxation inspectors. In addition to taxation, there are the issues of business registration, licences, certification, permissions for use of specialised equipment, insurance, and matters relating to superannuation.

Principals

There are a multitude of compliance requirements that apply to the principals of a healthcare practice; for example, codes of conduct, registration with various boards or colleges or professional associations, compliance requirements for referrals, and professional development.

Personnel

Compliance matters relating to personnel include: legislation, employment conditions, salaries and wages, workplace health and safety, insurance, professional development and training, performance appraisals or reviews, and confidentiality policies.

Services

In terms of patient services, there are a range of compliance matters to be addressed: medical procedures, patient education, consent issues, confidentiality and privacy, and control of infection.

Risk management

Risk management involves identifying the different types of risk a healthcare practice faces in conducting its business. It also involves identifying preventable and predictable risks and developing practical strategies to reduce the likelihood of these risks occurring in the practice. The connection between risk and compliance management is that compliance management identifies the obligations and requirements and then uses risk management techniques to manage the response.

Insurance

Professional indemnity insurance is a vital requirement for every healthcare professional, as is other insurance cover and workplace health and safety procedures and policies.

Information technology

Information technology is a vital requirement for any functioning and successful practice. There must be an emphasis on confidentiality, record security, software upgrades, personnel training, and website security.

Corporate governance

Finally, corporate governance—which relates to the overall management of the healthcare practice—is subject to compliance. Successful corporate governance ensures that decision-making and control mechanisms are carried out systematically and effectively. Such procedures are subject to review and are required to meet specific requirements established by organisations, government, and professional bodies.

It is essential that healthcare practices maintain a compliance register and implement a management program. The register contains details of the requirements of organisations such as the Australian Taxation Office, professional industry bodies, the *Privacy Act 1988* (Cth), the *Competition and Consumer Act 2010* (Cth), and the *Corporations Act 2001* (Cth). The compliance register prepares and maintains key legislative and regulatory requirements applying to the practice and is associated with the compliance management program that involves all practice personnel.

The management program ensures that all staff are trained in compliance matters and are aware of the procedures to be followed when compliance has been breached. The register also records the breach of compliance requirements and any appropriate action to be taken.

In summary, there are a host of compliance requirements for all those who work in the healthcare industry, including those seeking self-employment. Failure to take these into consideration is not acceptable and those wishing to consider self-employment must investigate the impact of compliance requirements on their practice.

Reasons not to seek self-employment in the healthcare industry

This chapter ends by focussing on five reasons to avoid seeking self-employment in healthcare. Patients will not be helped by professionals who are self-employed for the wrong reasons.

Wealth

Self-employment should lead to the accumulation of personal wealth; however, if the only objective in being self-employed is money then the decision to enter this type of employment is for the wrong reasons. Any wealth accumulated by the self-employed healthcare operator is the result of two factors: the number of patients and the fees per patient. The number of patients your practice attracts is directly related to the quality of your services, your ability to attract patients to the practice, and your success in providing patient services.

Status

Being self-employment in healthcare has a position of status within our society. Again, attaining a position of status is not a reason to establish a practice nor is it guaranteed unless it is deserved. The important factor here is the quality of the healthcare services you offer your patients.

Freedom

Self-employment in the healthcare industry provides an opportunity for flexibility and freedom in terms of time and management. Yet, a successful practice may produce the opposite: further demands may be made on your time, services, and expertise. Despite these demands, long-term job satisfaction is important and this is key in providing quality care for patients. Freedom can also exist in the sense that the professional is free to decide what services to be offered and the quality of those services.

Power

Healthcare self-employment represents a position of power within the community. All professionals in healthcare have certain elements of power for the simple reason they are providing care for patients who have an inferior knowledge of medical matters to themselves. The pursuit of this power is not a reason to enter self-employment. In fact, many soon come to the conclusion that the position of power carries a high degree of responsibility and demands. Success can lead to power but success is determined by the number of patients a practice has, the quality of care, and the success in delivering that care.

Pressure

Seeking self-employment in healthcare as a result of pressure from families, friends, or professional colleagues is unwise. Obtaining advice on your employment options is important in determining the best career option for you; entering into self-employment because of pressure from others is unacceptable.

This concludes Chapter 1. Consider the points we have raised about whether self-employment is an appropriate choice for you and your professional development. Ask yourself: at this stage, do you have any thoughts on starting a healthcare practice? We suggest that you read the checklist below to encourage your thought process relating to entering an independent practice.

Checklist: Factors influencing self-employment

Assessment of factors (1 = little importance, 10 = most important)

Question	Assessment/Answer
Consider and list your personal characteristics and qualities. Assess whether these qualities are appropriate for the various options regarding employment as a healthcare professional.	
What are your personal and professional qualities that would be considered a strength in a practice? What are your personal and professional qualities that would be considered a weakness in a practice?	
How important are the personal and professional qualities of healthcare professionals in determining practice image?	
How important are attitudes to compliance in determining practice image?	

Question	Assessment/Answer
How important is patience and tolerance in a healthcare professional seeking self-employment and why?	
Consider and list your reasons for entering into the healthcare profession. Then, rank each of these according to importance. Assess this against the reasons not to enter into self-employment.	
How would you describe your communication skills?	
What qualities suggest that you are an excellent "people person"?	
How can you meet the wide range of healthcare needs of your potential patients? What areas present a challenge to you and how can you address these challenges?	
Do you recognise the importance of patients being the "ambassadors" of your practice?	

Chapter 2: Self-Employment Options and Implications

Why was this chapter written?

The issues in this chapter are critical for healthcare professionals considering self-employment. This chapter discusses the various forms of self-employment that may be suitable for you. The decisions that you make concerning your future self-employment influences the development of any practice you are associated with and has a direct impact on your professional and personal lifestyle.

This chapter is divided into 16 subsections. We begin by outlining the various self-employment options before discussing business structure and why this is important for self-employed professionals. This is followed by a brief summary of the alternative self-employment practice options available to you. The final sections of this chapter examine issues such as implications for practices on business or practice development, use of business names, medical registrations, and advertising. The chapter concludes with a checklist on healthcare business practice options.

The 16 subsections of this chapter include:
1. Why was this chapter written?
2. What are my self-employment options?
3. Why is business structure important?
4. What are the legal considerations?
5. Option 1: Sole practitioner
6. Option 2: Associateship

7. Option 3: Partnership
8. Option 4: Company membership
9. Option 5: Starting your own practice with colleagues
10. Option 6: Joining an organisation or institution
11. Other issues to consider
12. Registering a business name
13. Healthcare practitioner registration
14. Advertising and signage
15. Making a decision
16. Checklist: Healthcare business practice options

What are my self-employment options?

Self-employment is an attitude and a way of life and can take a number of different organisational formats. The concept of self-employment depends upon the arrangements between the professionals in a practice. Self-employment options include:

- Option 1: being a sole practitioner
- Option 2: joining an established practice as an associate
- Option 3: joining an established practice as a partner
- Option 4: joining a corporate entity
- Option 5: starting your own practice with colleagues from the industry
- Option 6: joining an organisation or institution.

A *sole practitioner* is an individual who carries on a practice as a business in their own right as a proprietor whether in his or her own name or under a business name.

An *associate* is a self-employed professional who operates his or her own practice under the same legal framework as another associate; several associates may work together in a practice, each having their own system for identifying and billing patients. Members in the associateship tend to share costs—but not income—in a practice.

In general, various legislation at state and federal level defines *partnerships* in terms of a group of professionals carrying on a business in common with a view of producing a profit and sharing these profits in some way.

When an *established company* is involved, the individual professional may become a partner, an associate, or a salaried member of the group and still be regarded as "self-employed".

Traditionally, healthcare practices were operated by individual practitioners. Around the 1950s, practitioners developed the concept of practice partnerships and in the 1960s associateships began to increase in popularity. Towards the end of the 20th century, corporate ownership increased with public and private companies buying professional practices and contracting with professionals to provide and deliver services. None of these developments mean that the days of the sole practitioner have ended; rather, in the field of general healthcare practice we anticipate sole practitioners will continue to provide healthcare services.

Why is business structure important for self-employed professionals?

When starting into practice one of the first decisions you need to make is what legal structure to use. This is one of the areas where you need expert advice. The structure options include sole trader, partnership, company or trust.

There are at least five important reasons why business structures should be clearly identified:

1. Government at all levels need to know what business structure has been adopted because that structure impacts on the linkages between the government and the practice.

2. Patients must be aware of the business structure as this may have an impact on relationships between patients, practice, and staff.

3. Staff in the practice need to know whether they are being employed by an individual, a group of individuals, a company, a trust, or an alternative structure.

4. Management of the practice is influenced, to some extent, by the business structure in terms of their involvement in planning, marketing, financial performance, information technology, risk management, and the links between lifestyle and work for the professional.

5. Other businesses need to know the business structure of the practice they are dealing with in terms of supplying goods and services and accepting services from the practice.

Therefore, the business structure for a self-employed practice is important. Professionals that are establishing a practice need to decide what structure best serves the practice and those operating within the practice.

What are the legal considerations?

Self-employment options include employment as a sole practitioner, employment as an associate, employment within a partnership, employment in a company, or a combination of these. Regardless of the business structure adopted, it is essential that you seek specialist legal advice. It is imperative that you understand the immediate and long-term impacts of forming a particular structure. It is only through obtaining legal advice that you can be assured you are establishing your healthcare practice correctly from the outset. Specialist legal advice also provides you with information regarding the financial implications of the structure on the operation of the practice; taxation liability is only one of the many financial implications of a practice structure.

If you are in a partnership, you need to be aware of the relevant legislation at state and federal levels. In Queensland, for example, the relevant legislation is the *Partnership Act 1981*. This Act covers rules for partnerships and details of managing and dissolving partnerships.

Option 1: Sole practitioner

The sole practitioner structure is common within Australia, although an increasing number of professionals work in group practice rather than operating as sole practitioners. Sole practitioners may operate under a personal name or adopt a business name. For example, a medical professional may carry on a practice under the name "Dr Julie Wilson" or as "Regional Family Doctor". In the same way, a physiotherapist may have a practice entitled "John Wilson Physiotherapist" or as "Bayside Physiotherapy". Registration of the name of the practice needs to occur before the practice begins operating.

What are the advantages and disadvantages of this option?

The advantages of being a sole practitioner include:
- being directly accountable to your patients and to the profession
- having complete control over practice operations, assets, facilities, working hours, services to be offered, and staff employed
- the structure is relatively simple to establish
- the structure is relatively low cost to operate
- the possibility of income-splitting with a service company (discussed later in this chapter)
- taxation liability and superannuation benefits.

Despite these advantages, there are also some challenges to being a sole practitioner. The disadvantages of being a sole practitioner include:

- initial financial investment and ongoing investment for expansion or development has to be met by one person— you!
- lack of networking with other professionals
- responsibility for all actions and liabilities
- ongoing costs of equipment
- limited range of services
- taxation liability and superannuation disadvantages (for example, fringe benefits tax).

Option 2: Associateship

Associates are practitioners who share premises and expenses on an agreed basis but each practitioner generally retains the fees from patient consultations. In this sense, associates share infrastructure but do not share outcomes or their expertise in the delivery of services to patients.

What are the advantages and disadvantages of this option?

The advantages of being an associate include:

- each practitioner can specialise without having to consult with other practitioners. This means that there is a greater degree of autonomy and independence for the professional in providing healthcare services
- the structure is relatively simple to establish
- arrangements, management, administration, and use of infrastructure is effective and efficient as expenses are spread over a number of practitioners

- multidisciplinary healthcare practices and practices with sub-specialties could operate in this format
- ability to invest in equipment
- ability to practice in multiple locations
- taxation and superannuation benefits.

Despite these advantages, there are also some challenges. The disadvantages of being an associate include:
- liability may apply for actions of any practitioner
- taxation and superannuation disadvantages (for example, fringe benefits tax)
- the requirement to work closely with other professionals.

Option 3: Partnership

Partnerships are where two or three professionals come together with the intention (often through a formal agreement) to establish a practice, offer services to patients, and share management, administration, and profits. As noted above, the partnership may have a specific legal agreement that binds the operations and finances of the business as well as being structured within the terms of government legislation, such as the *Partnership Act 1981*. Government legislation addresses the following:
- rules determining whether a partnership exists
- conditions that apply to limited partnerships
- responsibilities and liabilities under a partnership
- dissolution of a partnership.

Any partnership agreement should be prepared by solicitors and although examples of an agreement are available they are not reproduced here. From a management point of view, the following is relevant in preparing and designing a partnership agreement:

- identify potential areas of disagreement and have solutions to each built into the agreement
- ensure that the implications of the agreement are clearly understood by all partners; particularly in areas such as handling money, sharing profits, access to staff, access to patients, and general management matters.

What are the advantages and disadvantages of this option?

The advantages of a partnership are similar to those discussed above for sole practitioners and associates and include:

- the structure is relatively simple to establish
- the structure is relatively low cost to operate
- having access to fellow practitioners for discussion, networking, and stimulation
- sharing expenses and investments in infrastructure and technical equipment
- having greater freedom and flexibility in terms of working hours.

Despite these advantages, there are also some challenges to being a partner. The disadvantages of being a partner include:

- partners are liable for acts and omissions of the other partners in the partnership
- partners are liable for the legal and financial responsibilities of the other partners
- there may be difficulties with senior partners who may resist change and restrict a practice in terms of progress and development
- there may be differences of opinion on workloads, roles of management, use of staff, and the introduction of new or existing partners
- taxation and superannuation disadvantages.

Option 4: Company membership

Incorporation as a company is legally possible for many professions in Australia. A "company" refers to an entity that is registered as such under the *Corporations Act 2001* (Cth). The registration of a company is administered in Australia by the Australian Securities and Investment Commission (ASIC), which oversees and administers the legislation governing operations of companies. ASIC suggests the following steps be taken in establishing a healthcare company:

- decide on business structure: this may incorporate family trusts, associateships, and contract personnel
- decide on a company name
- register the company name
- decide on operating rules via a constitution: this must be agreed to by all parties in the company
- obtain necessary consent from all parties to the company structure
- submit an application for registration of the company to ASIC.

The Australian Taxation Commissioner has ruled that no division of personal income is permitted within a company. This means that, for example, a healthcare practice will have a nil residual taxation income after salary or bonuses and superannuation are paid to practitioners.

Another important point to note is that a company remains a separate entity and is distinguished clearly from the practitioners. The company has a separate bank account, employment agreements, salaries, insurance, and registration requirements. Below, we discuss a service company and the organisational and control advantages that this structure has from the point of view of management.

What are the advantages and disadvantages of this option?

The advantages of forming a company include:

- the structure represents the existence of a separate legal which can be continued indefinitely
- the structure may provide some protection for members in terms of their personal assets
- lower taxation rates and beneficial provision of superannuation (for example, the use of vehicles and equipment).

Despite these advantages, there are also some challenges to a company structure. The disadvantages of the company structure include:

- the cost of establishing and maintaining the structure may be relatively high in terms of legal fees and registration costs
- there are statutory requirements that apply to companies and these may be seen as an administrative burden.

What about forming a service company?

It is possible to establish a service company for any professional practice irrespective of the legal structure involved. The advantages of forming a service company is that the company is responsible for items such as:

- support staff salaries and salary-related expenses
- expenses associated with infrastructure such as buildings and improvements
- expenses linked to technical equipment, office facilities, and vehicles
- general overheads and operational expenses such as travel, accommodation, communication, promotion, and marketing.

In addition, the advantages of a service company include:

- The Australian Tax Commissioner allows actual expenses to be recorded against the service company and that allows such expenses to be charged to the practice with a selected mark-up percentage. This means that the service company makes a profit which can then be distributed to beneficiaries who are usually members of the practitioner's family. Thus, a service company assists in spreading income

- From a management point of view, using a service company for managing the costs of general services and infrastructure may have budgetary advantages and control advantages. A service company can be a unit associated with a practice covering all the expenses of keeping a practice in a position ready to deliver its services

- A service company may be a motivational tool given the opportunities of earning bonuses while enabling cost savings within the company.

The only disadvantages of utilising a service company is the cost of establishing and maintaining such an entity and the administrative burden linked to regulatory and legislative requirements.

What about corporatisation?

A recent development involving company ownership of a professional practice is corporatisation. This is where a public or private company purchases the practice and enters into an agreement with the professionals to deliver services for patients for a salary, plus bonus and other benefits. Ownership of the practice passes from the practitioner to the company. The benefits of this arrangement to the practitioner depends on the tax implications of the sale of the practice and the earning, allowances, and other benefits associated with this option.

For example, a group of associates may be prepared to sell their practice to a public company and become salaried professionals delivering the same range of services to patients as was available before the sale. While there are ethical reasons to ensure patients are advised of the change of ownership, there would be no differences in the quality of services provided.

Option 5: Starting your own practice

"What if I don't get along with the other professionals in the practice?"

This is a common concern and, unless you are a sole practitioner, you have to work with other professionals—as an associate, a partner, or as a member of a company. Compatibility between the parties is a potential problem when joining an established practice. A great deal of trust needs to exist between all parties in order for the practice to operate smoothly: the larger the group, the more difficult this may become.

An alternative self-employment option is for you, as an individual professional, to form a practice group with a group of professionals that you already know and trust. This does not eliminate the issues associated with working with other professionals, but may provide a more stable working environment if trust, compatibility, and professional understanding is present from the start. This is an alternative to the four options offered at the start of this chapter; however, you still have to work out the business structure of the group (i.e. an associateship or a partnership) and comply with the legal, regulatory, and registration requirements. It is essential that you seek legal advice before establishing your own practice group so there is a clear understanding between all members of the rights and responsibilities associated with this option.

Option 6: Joining an organisation or institution

Graduates may choose to enter the healthcare industry in a hospital or university setting; for example, a public hospital or teaching hospital but also have the right to conduct a private practice in that setting. It is important for those practitioners who choose this path to understand they also need to know and understand how this type of practice operates. It is a business and has all the opportunities, obligations, and issues of any private practice. All of the information in this book can be applied to a practice no matter what the practice environment is. By applying the principles of this book, it gives those practitioners who choose to work in the "right to private practice" environment the ability to really know their practice, both from a business perspective and as a provider of quality healthcare services.

Other issues to consider

Now that we have identified what your self-employment options are, you need to consider the other implications of self-employment. The following six areas should be considered:
- financial considerations
- planning for the future
- information technology issues
- risk issues
- compliance issues
- work-life balance.

Financial considerations

Whether you are in a small or large professional group, your financial performance is critical to your professional success and the ongoing survival of the practice: fees from patients have to be planned, expenses have to be controlled. Therefore, short-term and long-term financial performance is essential.

Planning for the future

Planning is directly associated with financial performance and is so important for anyone considering self-employment. Planning extends to all aspects of the practice: planning for patients, planning for personnel, and planning for all aspects of finance.

Information technology issues

A practice that operates efficiently and effectively has a successfully implemented IT system. Every practice should aim to have a paperless office that utilises electronic communication between patients and the practice, and between staff within the practice.

Risk issues

Operating a practice has various issues associated with risk. Unless you are a sole practitioner, the risk generally stems from reliance on other professionals to adequately plan for future success, to perform financially, and to work professionally and competently. These risks need to be recognised and action taken to ensure those risks are addressed in a positive manner.

Compliance issues

Legislative and regulatory compliance is an essential element in self-employment. Meeting compliance requirements is not an option: it is an essential component of any professional practice and must be a factor when deciding which self-employment option is suitable for you. Compliance is discussed in detail in Chapter 9.

Work-life balance

Any aspect of a professional's working life involves the consideration of work and lifestyle balance. It is vital that working hours, pressures, and stress are kept in check to allow time for professional development, community involvement, and personal life.

Registering a business name

Irrespective of the business structure of your healthcare practice, the practice normally has a business name to identify it in the marketplace; for example, "X Street Medical Practice" or using the personal name of the healthcare professional. This business name needs to be different from any other name used for a healthcare practice. Once registered, the business name is used to trade under for healthcare services.

In Australia, a federal entity is responsible for registering business names. The Australian Securities and Investments Commission (ASIC) is Australia's corporate and financial services regulator and all business names must be registered through ASIC. The website for ASIC is www.asic.gov.au: please visit this site and familiarise yourself with its content.

All businesses have taxation responsibilities in relation to applying for an Australian Business Number (ABN), producing business activity statements (BAS), registering for Goods and Services Tax (GST), and taxation requirements in relation to practice expenses. The Australian Taxation Office is the body responsible for these requirements and their website www.ato.gov.au has the relevant information including starting · and running a small business.

Healthcare practitioner registration

Healthcare practices need to be registered with an appropriate board. For example, medical practices have to be registered with the Medical Board of Australia.[2] Each healthcare registration has its own list of categories. For example, medical registration is under one of a number of categories such as General, Specialist, Internship, Special Purpose, Non-Practising, and Short Term.

The Australian Health Practitioner Regulation Agency (AHPRA)[3] provides regulation for 14 health professions across Australia under the National Registration and Accreditation Scheme. All healthcare practitioners must be registered through AHPRA. AHPRA manages the registration and renewal processes for health practitioners and students around Australia.

In Australia, boards are responsible for healthcare operations, have regulatory roles, and are there to ensure that quality healthcare is provided to our community. As such, boards have a function to investigate complaints and to take any disciplinary action against registrants if unsatisfactory professional conduct is identified.

Advertising and signage

The obvious reason for advertising and signage is to promote the practice and provide information for patients and potential patients. Advertising is generally for external promotional use and signage is generally used within the practice.

---

2   See www.ama.com.au.
3   See www.ahpra.gov.au.

The use of advertising needs to be exercised with caution. Most professions have some constraints on the use of advertising material. Where an advertisement appears for a healthcare practice:

- the healthcare professional's name must appear in the advertisement
- healthcare professionals must be associated with the business
- the business name must be cited in the advertisements
- the name of any business must be stated clearly in any advertisement.

In general, advertising is prohibited where the advertisement:

- provides information that is false or misleading and deceptive
- provides actual endorsement or testimonials about a practice or about individual healthcare professionals
- offers a discount or some other inducement to attract members of a community to health services
- refers to professional services provided by another person in a negative way
- offers a service which is known as being harmful to a patient in some way
- offers a service where the healthcare professional does not have the qualifications for that service.

Regulations and requirements for advertising and signage are designated to protect the public and also to protect self-employed professionals. There are specific guidelines for the advertising of regulated health services and these are set out clearly on the Medical Board website www.medicalboard.gov.au: *Guidelines for Advertising of Registered Health Services.*

Within the practice, signage can be used for:
- identifying the aims, goals, and objectives of the practice
- identifying the names of professionals and support staff. For example, name tags on doors, reception areas, and on walls in rooms used by patients. There should also be a noticeboard displaying photographs and names of all the professionals and staff in the practice. All staff should wear a name tag that is clearly visible
- outlining the range of information and facilities available. For example, in a patient lounge signage can be used to guide patients to the library, audio-visual material, use of internet to allow patients to gain more information on healthcare matters, and pamphlets and brochures for distribution
- community healthcare notices and patient meetings. For example, dates and times for a meeting of patients with children for a talk on children's illnesses
- displaying standard consultation fees, after-hours fees, home visit fees, and other fees associated with practice services
- displaying operating hours for each day of the week including weekends
- displaying contact details for the practice and contact details for outside business hours
- direct phone numbers for professionals within the practice
- health insurance and Medicare information.

Making a decision

This chapter demonstrates that there are a range of options for an individual seeking self-employment in the healthcare industry—each with advantages and disadvantages. Now, you need to figure out which option is right for you. A starting point is examining the opportunities that currently exist in the market. For example, you may have close contact with an established group of professionals who are in practice and seeking to expand operations by adding an additional professional or you may have a friend who graduated university with you and you are both seeking to establish a small group practice. Consider your options and identify the strengths and weaknesses as well as possible risks associated with each.

Checklist: Healthcare business practice options

Question	Assessment
Consider the advantages and disadvantages of the six options for self-employment discussed in this chapter. Which one do you consider is right for you and why?	
Consider the requirements for registration of the business name and for various practitioners. How will you ensure that these requirements are met?	
How will you use advertising and signage within the practice and externally? What improvements could be made to any existing advertising and signage?	

Question	Assessment
Should the current restrictions or constraints on advertising by healthcare practices be continued or should practices be free to advertise and promote their practices as commercial entities?	
Consider the impact of compliance on self-employment. How does this influence your decision as to what employment option is right for you?	

Chapter 3: Attracting and Retaining Patients

Why was this chapter written?

The issues in this chapter review how a healthcare practice can attract and retain patients and convert current patients to practice ambassadors who actively represent and support practice development. It is self-evident that attracting and retaining patients is essential for the survival of a practice. Patients generate fees and fees are required to meet (in simplistic terms) three major practice expenses:

- weekly and monthly costs and expenses including staff salaries
- annual costs to ensure that the practice remains in business including rent and leasing, practice insurance, registration, and licences
- financial rewards including salaries or bonuses.

This chapter consists of 16 subsections covering all aspects of attracting and retaining patients. We begin by discussing the factors which are important in launching or building practice numbers and retaining patients for practice development. The final section of this chapter looks at patient target numbers and this is where the cost and expenses associated with the practice each year have to be taken into consideration. This chapter concludes with a checklist to review what has been discussed.

The 16 subsections of this chapter include:
1. Why was this chapter written?
2. Attracting patients: the impact of location
3. Attracting patients: actions by professionals
4. Attracting patients: the role of practice staff
5. Attracting patients: the importance of external referrals
6. Building patient numbers: reputation and word of mouth
7. Building patient numbers: the impact of practice image
8. Building patient numbers: marketing
9. Building patient numbers: practice services
10. Building patient numbers: the importance of patient follow-up
11. Retaining patients: the practice as a continuing healthcare centre
12. Retaining patients: external activities
13. Practice ambassadors: internal referrals
14. Networking
15. Setting targets for patient numbers
16. Checklist: Attracting and retaining patients.

Attracting patients: the impact of location

An obvious initial decision to be made when establishing a healthcare practice is the practice location. This decision is influenced by your personal preferences and by the commercial considerations of establishing the practice.

Factors that may be considered when choosing the location of a practice include:
• the current healthcare practices located close by
• a rural or regional location due to patient demand
• a suburban location due to the preference of the professional as to where they (and their family) reside

- a location near the professional's existing residence. This is not essential; many professionals travel to a number of locations to practice
- the need for specialisation of practice services in an area; for example, child healthcare services or healthcare for the elderly. Government statistics can provide details of population groups and ages[4]
- a location that provides ease of access for patients in terms of transport and parking.

Once a location is decided, you need to turn your mind to the actual practice site. There are many options, including:
- a commercial office or building
- a dedicated building for healthcare services with your practice occupying a section of the building
- a hospital complex
- a stand-alone building
- a converted house (with the approval of local authorities).

Once a site is decided, you need to then turn your mind to other issues, including:
- the quality of the building. This is important for practice image and the ability to attract and retain patients
- potential layout of the building. This is important to allow your practice to be designed to meet your professional requirements. It is necessary to have facilities such as a separate reception area for patients, a patient lounge, interview rooms, rooms for staff and professionals conducting consultations

---

4   See Australian Bureau of Statistics: www.abs.gov.au.

- access to the building. This is important in terms of parking facilities for patients with their own vehicles as well as access to public transport.

The initial step in attracting and retaining patients is to select a site which meets the needs of potential patients. From here, you then have to decide what action you need to take to attract patients and retain patient numbers.

Attracting patients: actions by professionals

Initially, the professional responsible for key actions for your practice is likely to be yourself, unless you decide to join a practice with other professionals, in which case the ideas set out below can be shared by all involved. Before you begin to publicise your practice, you need to make a number of decisions, including:

- What are the values of the practice?
- What range of services will be offered?
- What days of the week will the practice be open?
- What hours of the day will the practice be open?
- How can patients contact the practice?
- How you will use IT and social media; for example, a practice website, Facebook, LinkedIn?

How do you go about publicising these services? Here are five suggestions:

- *Presentations*: These may be given to schools, community meetings, or to clubs. A presentation on a relevant aspect of healthcare could be combined with details of your practice location and services.
- *Articles*: These may be written for journals, community newspapers, or websites. An article on a relevant aspect

of healthcare could be combined with details of your practice location and services.

- *Selective advertising*: Selective advertising of your practice may be appropriate where it is in accordance with the guidelines set by the relevant medical colleges and associations. The advertising could appear in local newspapers or online and should provide specific details of services, days of operation, and location for the practice.
- *Networking*: Networking with professional or industry groups increases the spread of information and potential referrals about your practice.
- *Mail-out*: Electronic newsletters or email streams have almost replaced mail-outs as a means of attracting new patients. However, for some areas the postal services can still provide assistance in identifying potential patients. There is an opportunity to focus on particular demographics; for example, retirees and families. Some practices might choose to contact whole communities electronically or through a physical mail-out.

At this stage, it is important to emphasise the need for referrals to the practice from patients and other professionals. This is directly related to the use of networking for publicising your practice. In order to establish your practice's patient list, you need referrals from other professionals. This means that you need to contact these professionals personally and provide them with details of your practice and its services. This networking requires regular follow-up to advise the professionals of any changes in your practice and to remind these professionals that you and your practice are available for referral.

The above suggestions should be implemented before your practice has been established. The next section applies after the practice has been established and looks at the role of practice staff in building patient numbers.

Attracting patients: the role of practice staff

Staff are critical in launching and developing a successful practice. Increasingly, the practice manager is the person who has the responsibility of developing staff in a practice. It is vital to devote time and attention to support staff—and their training—to ensure that their actions, their attitudes, and their general approach to patients is in the best interest of your practice.

An important principle is for the professional to spend as close to 100 percent of his or her time on clinical consultations with patients; after all, this is why patients come to the practice. This means that every other aspect of activity within the practice should be undertaken by support staff.

For example, consider a situation whereby a practice allocates 15 minutes for a patient consultation. However, this 15 minute consultation does not represent the time that the patient is in contact with the practice for the following reasons:

- it could take 10 minutes for the patient to discuss appointment times and alternatives on the phone with staff
- it is likely that the patient arrives at the practice at least 15 minutes before the consultation
- the consultation itself takes 15 minutes
- it could take a further 15 minutes for the patient to finalise arrangements after the consultation for a further consultation and payment of fees.

This means that of the total time the patient is actually communicating with the practice (55 minutes), 27 percent of this is time with the professional and the remaining 73 percent is time with practice staff either before or after the consultation. Therefore, there are several opportunities for staff to positively engage with patients. If this is not recognised, there is the risk that staff act as a barrier to practice development through their attitudes and actions.

Consider the following staff duties and how these could impact on your practice:

- Telephone techniques are important. This is often the first impression that patients have of your practice and the technique that staff employ over the telephone are critical to how patients view your practice. Most staff need special training on telephone techniques and it is in the interest of your practice that this be achieved successfully.
- The ability to answer emails is of similar importance to telephone techniques. Again, this may be the first impression that patients have of your practice and is critical to the attitude of patients.
- Collection of information from patients is done by practice staff. This information is personal and clinical and how this is carried out is important for your practice. Confidentiality and privacy issues needs to be considered.
- Registration with the practice needs to occur for every new patient. This registration process for new patients is completed by practice staff and how this is undertaken has an impact on the attitudes of patients to your practice. Confidentiality and privacy issues need to be considered.
- Practice information and details are constantly referred to by staff. This information is required to be given to the patient and to other interested parties (for example, referring professionals) and this needs careful attention in order to promote practice quality and image.
- Face-to-face contact by staff when the patient attends the practice for a consultation is vital. How staff deal with this situation is important for practice image and reputation.

The systems that are implemented in your practice are directly related to the role of the support staff. There is an ongoing trend towards a "paperless" office meaning that records are maintained in electronic form. A range of computer software programs are available; for example, Best Practice Software Pty Ltd, Genie Solutions Pty Ltd, HCN-Pracsoft, Stat Health Systems Pty Ltd, and Houston Medical Australia Pty Ltd. The MSIA[5]—Medical Software Industry Association—and Medicare list most of the healthcare software companies in Australia, so investigate these options and find the one that is right for your practice.

Most practices are computerised and their software includes clinical as well as administrative software. This gives practices the opportunity to work in a paperless environment where clinical and administrative records, results, referrals, and communications are online. Patient electronic records contain personal details, clinical information, and details of consultations, tests and results.

Some practices have the ability to allow patients to register online, make appointments online, and even communicate with the practice and the practitioner online. The commitment to using technology to maximise practice outcomes demonstrates to patients that the practice is at the cutting edge of services delivery.

This feature—the use of technology in a practice—is mentioned several times in other areas in this chapter as an indication of both efficiency and practice image.

Attracting patients: the importance of external referrals

Successful healthcare practices rely on external referrals: these are referrals from other practices and professionals within the healthcare

---

5   See www.msia.com.au.

industry. Specialist practices rely on referrals to establish and build their practices. In Australia, it is necessary to have a referral to a specialist if you wish to claim any of the costs of seeing that specialist from Medicare and the health insurance funds. Referrals come from healthcare practitioners with the recognised rights to refer patients and this can include all medical practitioners, dental practitioners, and a number of other healthcare practitioners; for example, physiotherapists and optometrists.

External referrals are critical for practice growth and development. Networking is important in this process as it allows you to focus on practices and industry professionals, which have the potential of referring patients to your practice. It is essential that these practices and individuals have full knowledge of your practice, its staff, contact information and operating details, and are aware of the range of healthcare services it provides. External referrals can be important in general practices offering specialised services as well as most allied health practice.

Building patient numbers: reputation and word of mouth

To a certain extent, the reputation of a healthcare practice is based on the outcomes of patient consultations. However, the reputation of your practice depends on more than this: it depends on the total experience of patients in contact with your practice. Therefore, support staff have an important role in this exercise. For this reason, it is important that staff be fully trained in dealing with patients and representing your practice.

It is also valid to say that practices gain patients through word of mouth—referrals and recommendations from patients and other healthcare professionals is important in building patient numbers. However, what is often forgotten is the fact that patients who are happy with a practice cannot recommend a practice without knowledge of the practice: its structure, organisation, and services. For this reason, if you wish to encourage patients to recommend the practice to others, it is important that all patients have knowledge of the details of the practice.

Imparting this knowledge can be as simple as having an up-to-date website or giving hand-outs to patients that provide details of the healthcare professionals, support staff, services, the practice's mission statement and vision for the future, as well as details of location, hours of operation, and other essential information.

Practice culture

The practice culture underpins the delivery of service in every area of the practice. The practice culture is supported by the mission statement and the vision for the future of the practice. It is important to understand the difference between the mission statement and the practice vision. A *mission statement* relates to what the practice is about and a *practice vision* is about what the practice wants to become.

The key questions relating to a mission statement are:
• What do we do?
• For whom do we do it?
• What is the benefit?

A practice vision describes how the practice looks if it achieves its mission statement. This information about the practice should be supported by a practice website containing videos and visuals of the practice, photographs and information about staff, details of the practice's mission statement and vision, information sheets on healthcare issues, as well the use of business cards and brochures that can be given to patients to use in their referral.

Building patient numbers: impact of practice image

The key aspects of image building can be summarised as follows:
- communication with patients needs to be of the highest quality
- patients must be treated as individuals not as numbers within a system
- the time a patient spends waiting for their consultation in the practice should be kept to a minimum
- any special needs of patients must be recorded and recognised
- each practice should develop a team effort for patient care
- practices should offer a total healthcare service for patients to meet needs of particular patient groups: this would depend on the type of practice you have
- the layout of the practice should enhance the image of the practice: there should be a reception area that is separate from the patient lounge to ensure confidentiality and privacy is guaranteed for communication between staff and patients.

It is worth emphasising the issue of waiting time that a patient may experience when arranging a consultation. This "time wasting", as it is often referred as, may begin when the patient first contacts a practice to arrange a consultation time. Delays can then occur during the registration process, while waiting for the professional in the practice, and while waiting for actions following the consultation. A major effort needs to be taken by all staff to reduce this waiting time as it can be a significant deterrent to practice image.

If these aspects are implemented, the outcome increases the linkages between patients and the practice—sometimes referred to as "bonding" between patients and the practice—for the benefit of the practice and to ensure long-term communication between patients and the practice.

Building patient numbers: marketing

Practices can successfully increase patient numbers if they decide to market their practice services. Many practices develop a specific marketing plan and use external advisors for this. Such marketing plans can include the practitioners' qualifications and expertise, the services offered by the practice, the standard of care, and the commitment of the practice staff. These plans give a practice the opportunity to work with a set of strategies and be able to measure the results though increases in patient numbers and services. The whole practice can become involved in marketing and can have a sense of achievement when goals are met.

Building patient numbers: practice services

The starting point in determining the services to be offered by your practice is the expertise of the professionals working there. Establishing and maintaining high-quality healthcare services is essential in ensuring that the practice attracts and maintains patients. It is self-evident that your services are the reason for patients to be attracted to your practice. Therefore, this area is worthy of close, detailed, and continuing attention.

What follows are a number of ideas that could be considered:

Identify the common needs of potential patients

Work with staff to identify the needs that are common to all of your patients, such as:

- skilled and competent pre-consultation interviews and/ or tests, care-plans, support services provided by support staff with appropriate experience and qualifications
- a caring approach by all staff
- confidentiality and privacy to all records and communications

Identify special needs of potential patients.

As well as the common needs listed above, there needs to be a focus by all staff on the particular needs of each patient, such as:

- retirees: special access facilities and specific consultation times
- single parents: special facilities, specific consultation times, and support staff who may provide childcare during the consultation
- working families: specific consultation times and support staff who may provide childcare during the consultation
- teenagers and young adults: specific consultation times to meet needs of school or university commitments
- patients with English as a second language: special provision made for use of an interpreter
- patients with particular ethnic backgrounds and cultural needs: staff to understand different cultures and the implications for communication, treatment, and advice
- practices may offer "specialised services". For example, there may be sub-specialties within a particular practice: in general practice, the sub-specialty might be industrial medicine or travel medicine; in other specialties, the particular type of physician, surgeon, or psychiatrist might have a specific area in which they work.

Add value to services

The practice should "add value" to consultation services for patients. This will likely come about as a result of:

- being innovative in communicating with patients
- hiring and training staff with the highest qualities and competencies
- ensuring staff maintain a positive attitude towards patients
- instilling the importance of patient linkages into staff; in other words, knowing patients, knowing each

patient's history—including family details, workplace, general lifestyle

- ensuring that patients are aware of the full range of practice services available
- adding new services to the practice as required to meet patient needs.

Offer multidisciplinary services

Ensure that the range of services offered are different from other practices by implementing multidisciplinary services:

- Utilise the resources of registered nurses. These nurses could offer specialist services—such as mental health treatment or services for those with disabilities—meaning the practice offers more than what is normally regarded as "healthcare service" from a practice
- Incorporate specialist healthcare services into your practice—such as occupational therapists, physiotherapists, speech pathologists, chiropractic services, podiatry services, services associated with audiology, and medical imaging. These services do not have to be available on a full-time basis: the key is to have them available for patients.

C.R.E.S.T

Develop an acronym to represent the interests and focus of your practice. As one example, C.R.E.S.T could be used:

C : Communication with patients, staff, and the community

R : Respect for self, patients, staff, professionals, community

E : Excellence in action, dedication, care, and achievement

S : Service for patients, their families, community, and the environment

T : Talent and training to achieve excellence in healthcare services.

Building patient numbers: the importance of patient follow-up

In this section, "patient follow-up" does not refer to clinical requirements; we are discussing ongoing contact with patients after the consultation has been completed. Generally, this is not a common practice: once the patient has been treated, there is usually no further contact by the practices unless the patient initiates contact.

We recommend this be changed so that once the consultation is completed arrangements can be made for ongoing contact between the patient and practice for the following reasons:

- ongoing contact demonstrates that your practice is concerned with the ongoing treatment and welfare of patients
- ongoing contact provides opportunities for further treatment and encourages patients to seek such treatment
- ongoing contact provides opportunities for feedback from patients on past treatments and future expectations of treatment
- follow-up provides opportunities for bonding between patients and the practice: this is important from the point of view of your practice being seen as a continuing healthcare centre.

There are two issues to be considered when implementing follow-up with patients in your practice:

1. How and when should contact be undertaken?
2. Can an ongoing plan of contact between patient and practice be developed over time?

In line with the suggestion already made that healthcare professionals should restrict their activity to consultations and procedures with patients, it follows that patient follow-up should be a task delegated to an appropriate staff member; one with key communication skills who appreciates the importance of maintaining contact with patients. It may be advantageous for a staff member to have some clinical training.

An alternative to an individual staff member providing this follow-up service would be a team of staff. An advantage of using a team is that the skills of a number of staff can be used to undertake ongoing follow-up.

How the follow-up is performed is open to debate: telephone contact, patient group meetings, and online contact are three possibilities. There are options within these possibilities to meet the needs of the patients and practice.

It is important to have a system and a plan in place to cater for:
• when the follow-up will commence
• what topics will be discussed during the follow-up
• how often should follow-up be initiated
• the extent to which patients can be involved in the follow-up by developing questions ask of professionals.

The more that patients are actively involved in the exercise, the greater the benefit of follow-up to both practice and patient.

Retaining patients: the practice as a continuing healthcare centre

Chapter 1 discusses the notion of the practice becoming a centre for healthcare. This concept is critical in ensuring patients retain links with your practice. Any independent practice has the potential to become a centre for patients and potential patients who are seeking specific healthcare services and may also seek information and advice on healthcare matters.

For this to become a reality, the following issues need attention:
• training of non-clinical staff in healthcare service matters and techniques to be used in assisting patients with

healthcare information: this can be regarding procedures, financial matters, use of equipment, expectations and external services

- healthcare information made available to patients by way of publications, brochures, journals, books, audio visual material, and online information. The practice should have the facilities for this information to be available to patients in the patient lounge
- clinical staff—including registered nurses—to provide healthcare services, advice to patients, and patient education
- the existence of information and advice needs to be strongly publicised among patients to promote referrals and recommendations.

The concept of the practice as a healthcare centre can extend beyond providing patients with information to the organisation of seminars, group discussions, or meetings between patients and professionals on specific healthcare issues; for example, a seminar for parents with young children. This notion is closely linked to ensuring that patients remain connected to the practice for the long term.

Associated with these activities is the introduction of a practice newsletter, mail-outs, and a practice website. A practice newsletter is a useful way of ensuring that the current patient list is kept up-to-date with the goings on of the practice. The newsletter is geared specifically to the practice and provides, for example, details of the practice, its staff, and its services. The newsletter could be sent out to patients via mail or email. A regular mail-out is another option to use to provide information to patients. The mail-out could cover specific topics at particular times of the year as well as including the details of the practice.

Websites are an integral part of today's healthcare practice. They can be used to provide information to patients on healthcare matters and promote the services the practice offers. Many websites allow for patients to communicate with the practice, make appointments, and download relevant information. Some websites include videos clips of the practitioners being interviewed or performing procedures. Sometimes satisfied patients are interviewed and this is additional practice promotion.

In summary, these three options—the newsletter, the mail-out, and the website—are important tools in encouraging patients to maintain links with the practice and to provide referrals and recommendations.

Retaining patients: external activities

Some practices become involved in external activities that help retain patients. Such activities can include visiting nursing homes, workplaces, and schools. These visits can involve providing healthcare services, giving lectures, and providing healthcare information on matters of community health. Some practices might also work with community organisations within their local area. All of these external activities have a direct impact on reputation of the practice and contribute to retaining current patients and obtaining patients in the future.

Practice ambassadors: internal referrals

The aim of successful healthcare practice management is to ensure that patients gain maximum satisfaction from each consultation. Satisfied patients produce "practice ambassadors": patients who refer your practice to others. However, there are two major barriers associated with the actions and attitudes of practice support staff which may negate that aim:

- waiting time faced by patients at several stages of the consultation process
- lack of assistance on matters associated with the consultation.

Waiting time

It is common for patients to have to wait before, during, and after the consultation. Initially, patients may face long waiting times merely to obtain a consultation. When they arrive at the practice, they may face further waiting time. If any follow-up is required, there is often further waiting time associated with that. This can become a source of frustration for patients. Practices need to have a system in place where patients are kept informed about waiting times. Appointment scheduling needs to consider the patient as well as the practitioner. Keep in touch with patients via text message or phone so they need not be kept waiting at the practice. Use little things to make their time in the practice easier; for example, coffee vouchers. Train staff to be constantly aware of the presence of patients in the waiting room or patient lounge.

Lack of assistance

Lack of information or clear advice may also be a problem for patients when they visit a practice. If patients are required to visit another healthcare institution, such as a hospital, lack of advice on what is required may frustrate the patient. Once again, practices need to have systems in place to alleviate this problem. This may include implementing a checklist for the information patients need to provide for any follow-up referral to another practitioner or government service, hospital procedure, or medical testing. It is important that patients feel they have been given every assistance from a practice to allow the patient to feel they have all the necessary information.

These two barriers do not exist in every practice and the experience of one patient may be different to the next. Patients can generally be divided into three groups:

1. patients who are mostly satisfied with the consultation experience and support the practice
2. patients who are antagonistic towards the practice as a result of the two barriers
3. patients who have mixed feelings towards the practice.

The *first* group are likely to encourage others to attend the practice and become ambassadors for the practice. The *second* group are the opposite: they are actively negative towards your practice and would not recommend it to others. The *third* group, while not negative towards the practice, may not actively encourage others to attend the practice.

The aim of any practice should be to encourage the creation of the first group—the practice ambassadors—as they are supportive of the practice and actively encourage others to attend the practice. This can be achieved by ensuring that support staff and professionals do everything in their power to provide patients with information, answer patient questions, reduce patient waiting time, and create an environment which is positive towards generating patient support.

Networking

Networking is the process of bringing individuals and organisations within the healthcare industry and community together for the exchange of ideas, obtaining knowledge, applying innovations, and meeting key industry contacts. Networking means working with people in a positive way to ensure that recommendations and referrals flow into your practice from these contacts. Practice networks may involve a wide range of people such as staff, patients, professionals, advisors, academics, government personnel, and business and commercial leaders. Networks may also involve organisations such as other healthcare practices, suppliers, community interest groups, government departments, industry organisations, and associations.

Networking has the following benefits:
- builds on the ability of your practice to meet the needs of patients
- creates bonds of patients to your practice
- increases your practice image by identifying your practice as a leader in the community
- provides stability through growth in patient numbers, economies of scale, efficiency, and improved profit margins
- contributes to long-term sustainability
- assists with the strategic direction of the practice
- provides a network within and external to your practice which ensures there are management benefits as well as professional benefits to the practice
- leads to an accumulation of knowledge and industry contacts
- increases the awareness of practice management techniques
- provides a mentoring system for the benefit of healthcare professionals and support staff
- encourages practice staff to be involved in the delivery of quality healthcare as a team
- may help to establish a Board of Advice.

A Board of Advice can provide your practice with a useful networking tool. As previously discussed, the Board is a group of professionals who provide advice to your practice without necessarily having any responsibility or control over practice operations. Board members provide advice on practice direction, patient matters, and organisational matters. Using your Board of Advice as a networking tool allows you to bring together your professional advisors and through them discover a completely different set of people to connect with and ideas to explore for the benefit of the practice.

Setting targets for patient numbers

It is important to set targets for potential patient numbers. This is a critical aspect of financial planning and ensuring that the practice remains financially viable. The target number of patients is directly related to how the practice operates. One of the first decisions to make is the number of patient consultations per professional per hour: will patient consultations be 15 minutes, 30 minutes, 1 hour or longer? This decision impacts on the number of patients targeted each day and the total fees to be raised through patient consultation.

What follows is an illustration to be used as a basis for calculating patient numbers.

Patients per consulting hour	4–5
Patients per professional per week	150
Patients per professional per day	30
Patients fees per consultation	$50
Fees per professional per hour	$250 (based on 5 patients per hour)

This example can be adjusted depending upon the length of consultation time and the proposed fee per patient. This allows you to estimate a figure representing the total amount of fees generated per week per professional. However, allowances have to be made for staff salaries and all costs associated with maintaining the practice. These matters are looked at in Chapters 7 and 8.

Checklist: Attracting and retaining patients

Assessment of factors (1= little importance, 10 = most important)

Factor	Assessment/Answer
How important is practice location in attracting patients? What could be done to improve the location of your practice or what would be the ideal location for a new practice?	
How can practice staff be used to keep patients connected to the practice?	Provide three roles: 1. 2. 3.
How would you rate practice reputation as a factor in retaining patients? What can be done to improve the reputation of your practice?	
How could you improve your image to assist you in attracting patients?	Provide three methods: 1. 2. 3.

Factor	Assessment/Answer
Do you have in mind specific practice services that could be offered to attract patients? Have you thought about how these services could be expanded in the future?	
How important is regular patient follow-up as a factor in retaining patients? What actions do you need to implement to achieve this?	
Do you believe you could convert patients to practice ambassadors? What actions would be important to convert your patients to such ambassadors?	
Do you anticipate barriers to patients remaining associated with the practice? What barriers might these be?	
List 3 actions which could help convert your practice into a healthcare centre.	1. 2. 3.
Formulate a plan to target patient numbers.	

Chapter 4: Patient Satisfaction

Why was this chapter written?

The content for this chapter draws heavily on the research undertaken for our previous book written for healthcare professionals: *Successful Practice Management: Exceeding Patient Expectations*. In the twelve chapters of that book we reviewed the major barriers faced by patients during the seven stages of the consultation process.

The seven stages of the consultation process are as follows:
1. patient referral and registration
2. management of patient healthcare information
3. the patient's attendance at the practice
4. pre-consultation procedures
5. consultation with the clinician
6. post-consultation procedures
7. post-consultation follow-up.

The barriers to patient satisfaction at each stage of the consultation process are as follows:
1. Excess waiting time
2. Problems related to gathering information (clinical or personal)
3. Lack of information by the practice

4. Layout of the practice leading to problems of confidentiality
5. Failure in administrative procedures
6. Failure to utilise technology
7. Negative staff attitudes
8. Failures in consultation with clinicians.

It is important for healthcare professionals wishing to establish a new practice or join an existing practice to recognise that these barriers have existed in the past and are likely to exist in the future unless sufficient action is taken. It is important to note that patients assume (quite correctly) they will have complete satisfaction from each consultation given the level of professional skill, competence, attitude, and experience of the clinicians. However, each consultation involves more than contact with clinicians—patients also have significant interactions with practice staff. Therefore, it is important for practice owners to be aware that patient satisfaction involves both practice staff and clinicians.

Patient satisfaction involves every person in the practice and every stage of the patient journey. It is a critical factor in any healthcare practice and should be an integral part of the culture of the practice. A practice culture reflects the way the practice operates: one that is based on shared values and beliefs and how it treats its employees, its patients, and the wider community. Addressing the barriers to patient satisfaction gives the practice the opportunity to improve its relationship with patients and referrers and has a significant impact on financial success and practice growth.

This chapter consists of 10 subsections addressing the barriers to patient satisfaction and provides practical advice in terms of implementing procedures to eliminate these barriers and maximise patient satisfaction.

The 10 subsections of this chapter include:
1. Why was this chapter written?
2. Excess waiting time

3. Problems related to gathering information
4. Lack of information by the practice
5. Layout of the practice leading to problems of confidentiality
6. Failure in administrative procedures
7. Failure to utilise technology
8. Negative staff attitudes
9. Failures in consultation with clinicians
10. Checklist: Maximising patient satisfaction

Excess waiting time

A common complaint voiced by patients is the waiting time associated with the consultation. This waiting time may arise as a result of:

- time delays in obtaining a clinician consultation
- delays in completing administration or registration arrangements by practice staff
- waiting time prior to each consultation with a clinician
- further waiting may be associated with post-consultation procedures.

Some of the problems associated with these waiting times may be overcome by the use of effective and efficient electronic communication methods. For example, if patients use email or online registration to register with your practice this can eliminate some delays compared to the use of hard-copy forms. This exercise is an effective and efficient use of professional time and every effort should be made for professionals seeing patients to maintain a budget of time and ensure that this budget is met.

Problems related to gathering information

Personal and clinical information needs to be obtained from the patient in order to have an effective consultation with a clinician. Where a patient has been referred to your practice by another clinician, both the referral and patient information may be received from the referring clinician or personal information may come from the patients and clinical information from the referring clinician. There may be delays in gathering this information from patients if they are not notified in advance; for example, providing details of previous consultations or health problems.

The solution to the problems relating to gathering information is for practices to provide to potential patients in advance details of what personal and clinical information is required. Having prior knowledge of what information is required at the initial consultation allows patients to have this information available on the day and goes a long way to eliminating any delays. Any clinical information from referring clinicians should be made available at the time of the consultation.

Lack of information by the practice

Failure to provide patients with adequate information concerning their consultation is a major area of dissatisfaction. This problem may be caused by the failure of a referring clinician to inform the patient about your practice or by the failure of a referred practice to provide information to the new patient on various matters associated with their consultation. New practices must have a strategy to ensure that all patients become "ambassadorial" and actively encourage others to select your practice for their healthcare needs. This means that new patients must be completely satisfied with all aspects of their consultation.

The activities which can cause problems for patients include:

- failure to provide information about the practice; for example, services, method of operation, and personnel
- failure to provide information about alternative clinicians within your practice that are available to patients
- failure to give details of what information is required from patients at each consultation; for example, information from previous healthcare providers
- failure to provide information on the consultation procedure; for example, details of how the consultation will be conducted, whether patients will see a clinician within your practice or be referred to other practices or a hospital
- failure to provide information on costs of the consultation to patients prior to their visit to the practice
- failure to have effective communication between staff, professionals, and patients; for example, verbal communication is used with patients when written communication would be more appropriate
- failure to provide written information to patients on critical areas arising from their consultation.

All of these areas of potential patient frustration can be eliminated with planning and specific action. The following are examples:

- a printed information sheet providing details of your practice, staff, services, and professionals
- written instructions on procedures to be followed during each consultation
- written details of estimated consultation costs
- a variety of communication techniques, including use of electronic tablets to illustrate procedures and requirements.

Layout of the practice leading to problems of confidentiality

It is not unusual for patients to have complaints about the layout and location of practices. Common problems can include:

- confusion and lack of information concerning practice location making it difficult for patients to find your practice or arrange parking or public transport
- poor layout within the practice meaning that waiting areas are crowded causing discomfort, lack of confidentiality, and lack of satisfaction
- facilities in the practice are inadequate and inappropriate; for example, no facilities for refreshments, access to internet, or reading material which is up-to-date and appropriate
- the absence of a confidential interview room for patients
- there is a lack of colour or lighting meaning that the practice is not furnished attractively to calm patients who may be stressed prior to their consultation.

The key to successful layout is to provide patients with the space and facilities appropriate for their reason for attending at your practice. Patients who are waiting to see clinicians should be accommodated within a lounge area with appropriate facilities including refreshments, reading material, television, radio with separate hearing facilities, and a separate space for children.

Problems associated with location could be overcome by providing patients with a printed map with details of the location including entry, parking, public transport options, and contact phone numbers. These are straightforward solutions to problems that should not have arisen in the first place.

Failure in administrative procedures

Common problems can include:

- inefficient communication systems that frustrate patients trying to contact your practice and/or provide the practice with information required for the consultation
- failure to identify a staff member who is designated as a patient coordinator. This does not mean that the practice will necessarily have one full-time patient coordinator but rather have a staff member who is responsible for patient coordination
- confusion concerning consultations arrangements and registration due to lack of systems
- poor patient progression which means there is always a queue of patients and there may be significant delays in arranging consultation times
- lack of confidentiality in discussions with staff due to poor layout
- little, if any, explanation of consultation and clinical procedures to be followed meaning patients are unaware of what is to be achieved, what is happening, and what procedures are to be followed
- lack of assistance in arranging follow-up procedures such as surgery, hospital visits, and visits to other clinicians.

All of these problems can be overcome to relieve patients of frustration and dissatisfaction. There should be no difficulty in ensuring that practice systems are efficient, that arrangements for confidential interviews and registration are in place for new patients, and that patient progression and waiting time can improve.

Planning each consultation before a patient arrives ensures that the patient receives an explanation of clinical procedures and assistance with follow-up procedures. As noted previously, these explanations should be in written form. It cannot be assumed that patients automatically understand everything that is explained to them verbally. Generally, communication between practice personnel and patients should be in written form rather than verbally.

Failure to utilise technology

Patients expect practices, especially a new practice, to be at the forefront of technology in its facilities and systems. The use of technology needs to include a functioning and practical website that provides relevant practice and healthcare information and the use of electronic tablets in patient registration.

Common problems can include:

- failure to utilise technology in referral procedures or registration procedures
- failure to utilise technology in information-gathering
- staff that are not familiar with the latest technologies
- failure to utilise technology in patient follow-up procedures.

There is no reason for these problems to exist; the use of technology is the most appropriate method for referrals, registrations and follow-up procedures, and staff training on utilisation of technology is not optional. When hiring staff for your practice, understanding and utilisation of technology should be a key factor in the decision to hire. In addition, professional development programs for staff should emphasise the use of technology.

Overall, your practice should be at the forefront of technology in its operations, communication with patients, and general administrative procedures.

Negative staff attitudes

As noted earlier in this book, staff are the key assets of your practice. Staff attitudes have a direct impact on patients; staff should be expected to provide positive, caring advice and assistance to patients at all times. If staff do not meet these expectations, patients become dissatisfied. The practice needs to ensure that task-oriented and people-oriented staff are employed. Attitudes and behaviour should be a key factor when hiring staff. The methods of communication with patients should be a feature of professional development programs.

Common problems can include:
- Staff not having a caring or positive attitude towards patients: staff in a healthcare practice must possess a positive attitudes
- Staff not having personal knowledge of patients: it is essential that patient details be collected so that staff have an adequate knowledge of patients and their background and that this knowledge is shared amongst staff
- Staff having poor telephone techniques: the telephone is a major form of communication between patients and the practice and can be the first contact point. The practice should consider specific training and development in telephone techniques
- Staff having poor presentation: uniforms for all staff is an option but more importantly the quality of staff presentation should be at a level which represents the quality of the practice
- Staff having poor communication methods: poor interpersonal skills and body language often cause problems for patients. A variety of communication methods should be used by staff when communicating with patients. Communication can include verbal and visual communication, electronic communication, and

written communication. The practice should consider specific training and development in communication and positive body language

- Staff having poor listening skills: listening to patients is an important aspect of communication and needs to be emphasised by the practice
- Staff fail to recognise complex situations: a problem faced by staff is that their work in healthcare often involves unique and complex situations. Staff can fail to recognise the complexities of the consultation process and fail to explain these processes in detail to patients. This applies particularly where there are follow-up procedures outside the practice such as admission to hospital, surgery, admission to other practices, or referral to other practices. Explanations for these procedures are critical
- Staff that do not work in teams: patients may assume that a practice has implemented staff teams to ensure the practice operates smoothly. Teams can exist in a practice that only has a few full-time staff members: teams can be created with a combination of part-time and full-time staff. The use of teams mean that patients expect efficiency in welcoming them to the practice and undertaking registration and similar tasks effectively. Where teams obviously do not exist or where teams are operating ineffectively, this causes problems for patients.

All of the above problems associated with personnel can be overcome through training, guidance, and selecting staff initially who are caring and have a positive attitude towards patients employed within a healthcare practice. Careful selection of staff is essential to practice success.

Failures in consultation with clinicians

Patients assign the greatest value from a practice from their consultation with clinicians and the clinician's attitudes, skills, competence, and experience. Other administrative systems can lead to patient dissatisfaction and offset any satisfaction produced by the consultation. However, actions by clinicians can also lead to a decline in patient satisfaction. Common problems can include:

- Failure of clinicians to plan for each consultation: the obvious solution to this is for clinicians and staff to automatically assume that every consultation requires preliminary planning
- Failure of clinicians to communicate with patients in lay language: communication between clinician and patient in a consultation can be highly technical and there are problems associated with using such technical language
- Failure of clinicians to listen to patients: this is as important as communicating verbally with patients. Clinicians should avoid giving the impression that he or she is so busy they cannot allocate time to listening to patients
- Poor relationships between staff and clinicians: friction between staff and clinicians is a negative from the point of view of patients. Staff are employed to cooperate with and support clinicians and this should be evident through practice communication processes. Clinicians should aim to allocate 100 percent of their time to patients with all other aspects of practice administration allocated to support staff. If there is a failure to utilise staff for basic administrative processes, this is seen as a negative from the point of view of patients

- Failure by clinicians to explain the outcome of consultations: an important role of clinicians (and selected support staff) is to explain the outcome of consultations. Outcomes may be complex and clear communication between patient and clinician is required in order for this to be successful
- Failure to provide written reports: after a consultation, in addition to verbal explanations, patients should be given a written report of outcomes and recommendations. The practice should have systems in place to cater for this important task
- Failure to encourage patient interaction: successful healthcare practices ensure that patients interact with each other, members of the practice team, and external support options. This interaction should be encouraged by clinicians. This is part of the tasks of encouraging patients to link to your practice on an ongoing basis. In this way, patients become ambassadors of your practice and contribute to the growth of the practice.

This chapter includes a long list of potential problems for patients that may occur in your practice. All of these problems can be eliminated with careful planning and application of common sense approaches. There may be merit in identifying the key areas of potential problems and concentrating on these initially to ensure that they are quickly eliminated.

Checklist: Maximising patient satisfaction

Question	Answer
Can you identify a particular area in practice administration where you can reduce patient waiting time?	
How can patient waiting time be managed? What specific procedures or arrangements need to be set up to minimise the impact of any waiting time?	
Can you introduce procedures which would reduce the problems associated with patient data collection?	
How would you supply information concerning your practice and procedures to be followed to new patients? Do you see the importance of written communication for this exercise?	
Can you improve the practice procedures which would be appropriate for consultation procedures, registration, and costs?	

Question	Answer
Organising the layout of the practice to provide interview rooms and patient lounges involves cost: do you see this as a major problem or would the benefits exceed the cost?	
Is it unreasonable to assume that all new staff appointed to your practice are technology-competent? How can you ensure that knowledge of technology remains a key issue for all staff?	
Identify the staff attitudes that may create problems for patients. Do you see some of these attitudes as being more important than others?	
Do you feel you could cope with changing staff attitudes yourself or would it be appropriate to utilise an external human resource specialist?	
How would you deal with correcting problems created by clinicians?	

Chapter 5: The Importance of Staff

Why was this chapter written?

In Chapter 5 we focus on the importance of the qualities of the staff you employ in your practice. Practice staff represent you and your values. They become the face of your practice. They are often the first and last point of contact for patients. Therefore, we focus on the importance of hiring the right staff, the role of the practice manager, and staff development to obtain the best results for the whole practice—patients, practitioners, staff and the practice itself.

Each of the 14 subsections in this chapter focus on the qualities of the staff that are employed in your practice. Keep in mind that our emphasis is on assisting you to have the skills required to provide patients with quality healthcare services in your practice. We begin by discussing entrepreneurial attitudes and hiring staff to fill positions with specific and designated responsibilities—such as the role of the practice manager in staff selection and management—as well as the importance of hiring staff who are IT-literate. The remaining sections of this chapter focus on management skills, managing performance, and continuing self-development.

The 14 subsections of this chapter include:
1. Why was this chapter written?
2. The role of the practice manager

3. Hiring staff with entrepreneurial attitudes
4. Hiring staff to fill designated positions
5. Hiring staff who are IT-literate
6. Hiring staff and staff development
7. Promoting and developing leadership
8. Developing teams
9. Motivating and encouraging self-motivation
10. Management of performance
11. Staff as managers
12. Being positive: bring out the best in your staff
13. Checklist: The importance of staff
14. Checklist: Staff recruitment and employment

The role of the practice manager

Every practice should have a member of staff appointed to the position of practice manager. Regardless of the size of the practice, it is a business and it needs to be managed accordingly. One of the responsibilities for the practice manager is the overall management of staff and interactions with patients. This position needs to be taken seriously with the responsible staff member having basic knowledge of management.

Depending on practice size and the number of staff to be appointed, there may also be opportunities for specialist staff appointments such as:

- patient coordinator: responsible for meeting with new patients, recording the registration of new patients, and overseeing the delivery of patient care
- systems and records coordinator: responsible for all systems including patient records, financial information, and operating systems

- staff development officer: responsible for staff appointments, staff inductions, staff development in terms of training, and professional development.

Identifying the specific responsibilities for staff members are important as it impacts on the image of the practice. The aim is to create an image of a practice as one that is effective and efficient.

Hiring staff with entrepreneurial attitudes

The structure of your practice should aim to create an entrepreneurial organisation as outlined by the successful author Colin Turner[6]. Turner begins his book with an Introduction entitled 'The future belongs to the fearless, the innovative, and the entrepreneurial'. The ideas that Turner presents in his book can be applied to your practice; in particular, those relating to the appointment of new staff. Turner suggests that business success arises from executive insight, intuition, initiative, innovation, integrity, individuality and interdependence in applying these concepts to colleagues in teams. Turner develops the theme of creating entrepreneurial organisations and makes recommendations for the appointment of "ambassadorial alliances" and building entrepreneurial networks.[7]

Turner's ideas can be applied to new staff appointed to your practice who have daily opportunities to meet potential patients and to convert these patients into "practice ambassadors"

---

6   Turner, Colin. *Lead to Succeed: Creating Entrepreneurial Organisations.* UK: Texere Publishing Company, 2002.
7   See the definition of this term at: http://en.wikipedia.org/wiki/Entrepreneurial_network. See also the Stanford Entrepreneurial Network at: https://sen.stanford.edu/?.

via entrepreneurial networks. The concept of practice ambassadors is where new patients become ambassadors for your practice, encouraging others in the community to visit the practice as a patient, and therefore encouraging practice growth. To suggest that staff of the practice are only involved in "front desk" or administrative activities is an incorrect and misleading view. By encouraging initiative, innovation, and motivation, practice staff can take an entrepreneurial role in practice growth and development.

Ideally, newly-hired staff will have knowledge of the practice operations, confidence in the practice's future, and see their role as an important driving force in assisting the practice to achieve its growth potential. We have emphasised that support staff should release professionals of all major administrative matters to allow them to allocate 100 percent of their time to providing consulting services for patients. Staff with entrepreneurial attitudes and drive are essential to ensure that this objective is achieved.

Hiring staff to fill designated positions

While entrepreneurial qualities and attitudes are critical for staff employed in your practice, it is equally important for staff to be able to handle the specific responsibilities associated with designated positions. Staff must be seen as effective and efficient by patients and others associated with the practice. Newly-hired staff will require expertise in areas such as:
- responding to telephone enquiries from potential patients
- displaying knowledge of the practice, its services, professionals, location, contact details, and hours of operation
- responding to electronic queries from potential patients
- completing registration requirements and storing information of patients

- welcoming new patients who come to the practice for a consultation
- assisting with the management of patient recall and reminders
- facilitate any patient follow-up on behalf of the practitioner
- providing new patients with all information required prior to their consultation
- assisting professionals where required in preparing for patient consultations
- discussing costs of services with patients before they attend the practice
- processing fee payments following consultations
- maintaining an efficient front office in layout, organisation, and furnishing arrangements
- organising the patient lounge, special areas for children, provision of reading material, and refreshments
- assisting with the promotion of the practice with patients by way of brochures and business cards
- assisting with communication with patients and potential patients by way of handouts and signage
- dealing with suppliers as required, ordering supplies, keeping records of medical and non-medical supplies
- communicating with referrers, other healthcare practices, and other healthcare professionals
- dealing with representatives who may visit your practice.

The above list is not conclusive—each staff member's position requires an element of flexibility in terms of its responsibilities—but it does represent the basic requirements of staff in terms of their general knowledge of practice operations and ability to handle questions and queries arising from patients. This means that new staff need to demonstrate adequate previous experience in practice operations or that training has to be provided to them to achieve this knowledge. We suggest that all new staff undergo an induction process to ensure they have the opportunity to gain the knowledge of what is required in your practice.

Hiring staff who are IT-literate

Technology is now widely in use in healthcare practices throughout Australia. Any practice should ensure that systems are in place for effective and efficient operation of up-to-date technology and any staff appointed to the practice must be IT-literate. Staff whose qualifications do not include IT proficiency should be provided with training to upgrade their skills and knowledge.

Each practice should have specific policies and procedures relating to information technology. Some of the IT responsibilities in a practice environment include:

- record keeping: records within your practice should feature computer-based systems with the aim of being a "paperless" office. This includes all patient records, medical reports, and referrals as well as operational records
- specialist software programs: programs exist for healthcare practices for electronic medical records and practice administration, appointment booking systems, and patient billing; for example, Best Practice, Genie, Medical Director-HCN, Blue Chip, Houston Medical, Pracsoft, Zedmed, Shexie, Stat Health. Specialist training should be provided for staff who do not have knowledge of these systems
- security systems: these systems must be upgraded to the highest quality. It is essential to have effective computer software that ensures that the practice's information and records are protected from viruses and other potential technology failures

- communication: this communication between the practice and patients should largely be electronic, using email, online services, and SMS services
- appointments and registration: online appointment systems and registration online or via email should be used
- telephone contact: staff should be aware that some patients may not have access to electronic services and so contacting patients by telephone may be necessary.

Hiring staff and staff development

In this section, we provide a summary of strategies that should be developed and applied for new staff, hiring staff, and for staff development.

There are a number of issues to be considered:

- Use of contract services as opposed to hiring staff: Contract services for full-time, part-time, or temporary staff may be useful to a practice that requires assistance in administrative matters such as record keeping, financial operations, word processing, or preparing prescriptions. In addition, voice-recognition software programs are available and may result in the need for fewer full-time staff.
- Hiring experienced staff: There are benefits in hiring staff with experience in healthcare practice management. You may find that these staff members require significantly less training and direction than their less experienced counterparts. Consider having a mixture of experienced and inexperienced staff within your practice, as there is merit in being able to provide training and guidance to those with less experience.
- Finding potential employees: Sourcing potential employees depends on the particular circumstances of your practice:

options may include employment agencies, word-of-mouth, advertising, bulletin boards, journals, newspapers, and online.

- Interviewing potential employees: Interviews are a critical part of hiring the right staff for your practice. Interviews provide you with the opportunity to determine whether the qualities and skills of the applicant meets the needs of your practice and whether the applicant has the ability to communicate, the ability to exercise judgment, the capacity to problem-solve, the ability to think on the spot, and possesses the self-confidence and willingness to undertake training and learning on-the-job. In the interview, questions relating to age, gender, ethnicity, marital status, sexual orientation and disabilities are not allowed by law. Identify and ask key questions such as: why the applicants has applied for the position, what they see as their own strengths and weaknesses, their previous experience, what have they achieved in past positions, and what they expect to achieve in the position.

- Employment contracts: how staff are employed in a practice must comply with employment legislation; for example, the *Fair Work Act 2009* (Cth). It is always important to get advice from employment law professionals in order to have a suitable employment contract for your staff. Benefits for the individual staff member (financial and non-financial) as well as other conditions may vary depending on the individual and the position.

- Compliance requirements: There are a host of compliance requirements associated with employing staff within a practice and these must be followed. Examples of compliance relating to employing staff include privacy legislation, anti-discrimination legislation, occupational health and safety requirements, taxation requirements, and superannuation obligations. Many professional associations and colleges are able to provide advice to members in relation to employing staff.

This list represents a standard list of activities that apply to staff development:

- Each staff position has a clearly documented job description that details the responsibilities and skills required of the role.
- Each staff member has a clearly documented career path that lists the expectations and performance indicators of the role.
- Staff performance is regularly appraised and remuneration and promotion is based on performance.
- Standard operational health and safety regulations are implemented within the practice.
- In-house and external training for staff emphasises the importance of high-quality inter-staff communication as well as communication with external contacts.
- Staff training schedules are prepared that meet the needs of your practice. Staff training may be required for staff to cover key areas such as welcoming and handling patients, operating systems, record keeping, and (where a number of staff are employed) management of staff functions.
- Strategies for staff development are discussed and formally documented.
- The practice has a comprehensive practice manual that is updated regularly.
- Staff attitudes and communication skills are to be a reflection of a high-quality working environment that generates a positive image for the practice.
- All staff are encouraged to complete formal training awards, including IT skills and aspects of practice management.

It is important that time and effort be placed into the hiring and development of staff in your practice. After all, having high-quality staff ensures that your practice is heading in the right direction of achieving a good reputation and image in the healthcare industry, which directly relates to the practice's ability to be financially sustainable.

Promoting and developing leadership

Good leadership is one of the essential factors in the success of any business. In a healthcare practice, where you have a number of separate but integrated areas (clinical, reception, administrative, procedures) there is an opportunity and a need for leadership on many levels.

This section is divided into two components: promoting leadership and developing leadership by staff. The assumption is that the staff appointed to your practice have the characteristics and qualities which allow leadership to be developed. The major attributes of leaders are those with the ability to:
* maintain commitment
* gain respect from others
* continuously pursue ongoing learning
* be open to new ideas
* adjust to changing conditions
* seek to improve their attitude, knowledge, and skills.

Leaders are those who:
* are looked to for advice
* develop and implement new ideas
* take an active role in the life of the business community
* organise their time
* make plans
* learn from mistakes
* build on self-confidence
* deal with people effectively

- delegate
- share success
- are results-oriented
- develop and build up the self-esteem of staff by having confidence in them and by praising their achievements
- are excellent communicators with staff, explaining day-to-day activities and long-term goals without revealing confidential information
- delegate tasks to others when appropriate, assist where necessary, correct mistakes, and provide support
- maintain personal contact with staff members, working on the assumption that every person has different characteristics, different abilities, and different capabilities
- attempt to bring out the potential of each individual and build on their talents
- avoid negative analysis or criticism of individuals and focus on solutions to problems
- provide positive reinforcement wherever possible by building on positive achievements
- are active motivators who listen to others to learn about the practice and its strengths and weaknesses.

Leadership qualities can be developed by individuals but exactly how this happens and to what extent they are developed varies from person to person because of the nature of leadership. By understanding how leaders motivate people, leadership qualities can be developed.

Two important features of leaders are their ability to communicate and their ability to develop high morale. Leaders encourage positive approaches to change and encourage change through education, communication, and enthusiasm for staff achievements. This is attained by providing opportunities for staff to develop their own skills and competencies under the guidance of a leader who recognises and encourages their efforts.

We comment further on leadership when we discuss the roles of teams within your practice. Teams must have a designated leader to function effectively. Therefore, selection of this person is critical for the success of the team and your practice.

Developing teams

As we have discussed, healthcare practices have a number of separate but integrated areas involved in the delivery of patient services. These areas can include reception, administrative roles, clinical services, and healthcare practitioners. These areas form practice teams, each with their own skills and experience and they work together for the benefit of the practice and patients.[8]

It may initially appear difficult to establish teams in a developing practice because of the small numbers of staff involved; however, this need not be the case. While there may be only one or two full-time staff in your practice, there is no reason why teams should not be established by combining these staff with part-time or casual staff. In addition, external professionals (such as accountants, solicitors, consultants) can also join full-time staff in forming teams.

Teams are important for your practice's future. The use of teams within a practice brings together a range of skills from full-time or part-time staff who represent a diverse range of backgrounds, experience, and attitudes. An effective team are highly regarded by patients. For example, a practice team responsible for dealing with patients (greeting patients, coordinating patients and planning consultations) could include a full-time staff member plus a part-time staff member

---

8   Meredith, G and Sullivan, C. *Successful Practice Management: Exceeding Patient Expectations.* USA: Lulu Books, 2012.

with skills in administration, organisation, and communication. Similarly, a team responsible for practice systems could include a full-time staff member plus a systems consultant and an accountant. Flexibility in establishing teams is important and benefits your practice and its patients.

As for all systems within a practice, establishing and managing teams has to be planned. Consider the following points:

- Take the time to plan your teams. Specific team structure and tasks have to be nominated and identified as being significant for your practice.
- The tasks to be completed to achieve the objectives of your practice should be planned carefully and documented and agreed to by members of the practice teams.
- Reporting points during a specified time period should be nominated so that progress can be measured and reported effectively.
- Team activities should be reviewed and success documented. Any problems associated with team efforts should be recognised and dealt with appropriately.

Effective and efficient use of teams for various tasks within your practice results in significant practice rewards. This effective use of teams provides your staff with satisfaction in achieving results and overcoming particular problems that might be identified in your team planning exercise (as mentioned above).

Team leadership is an important aspect of team success. Team leaders are likely to be those staff members who can:

- grasp opportunities for change and upgrade services within the practice
- demonstrate high-quality communication skills
- generate enthusiasm amongst team members
- look for opportunities to expand patient numbers and practice growth.

The outcomes of successful team activities should be self-evident: any task that is allocated to the team should lead to success for team members and the practice. Teams should be a component of your practice, whether your practice is new or established.

Motivating and encouraging self-motivation

The key to any exercise of motivation is knowledge: ensuring staff understand what the practice is aiming to achieve and how that achievement is possible. An important point to remember at this instance is that "knowledge is power", which implies that those staff members that understand what your practice is trying to achieve will effectively work with you to improve the practice. The extent of this depends on hiring and motivating the "right" people when you make new staff appointments.

As a practice owner, it is important to realise that negative motivation through fear does not produce any sort of long-term results. These approaches can lead to resentment from staff and a negative approach to the practice as a workplace. Successful motivation results in staff who wish to succeed individually and who wish to see the practice succeed. The first step to achieving a workplace that is positively motivated is to understand how much knowledge staff have about the practice and its needs and operations. It may be necessary for you to arrange training sessions to explain how your practice operates: its strengths, its weaknesses, its future plans, and what is needed from its staff to ensure success. This approach is likely to mean that you are required to take staff into your confidence, particularly in the discussion of financial planning and future practice development. In order to do this you must have confidence in your staff and their ability to protect confidential information.

If staff feel they are part of a practice's success and are kept informed of the plans and operations associated with a practice, it is likely they will be motivated and proactive. Too often, there is a gap between the professionals who own and operate a practice and the staff who are employed within that practice. This gap can mean that much information—particularly financial information—is not made available to staff and therefore they are unclear on how your practice is to achieve success. For example, is there is any reason why staff should not be aware of the consultation fees for patients? Should staff be aware of the minimum number of patients required to "break even" and cover all costs associated with the practice?

The practice should have clearly established guidelines and standards that are made available to all staff in the practice. This way, staff not only know what the guidelines and standards are for the practice, but are able to identify their specific responsibilities in terms of dealing with patients and understanding the expectations of financial benchmarks. A financially successful practice is a practice that has a high quality of services and staff should be aware of this and be proud of achieving that success. Linked to practice success are promotions, further training, rewards, or other incentives—all of which can be used to motivate and encourage staff.

When incentives and rewards are offered to staff, consider offering staff alternatives to money, such as:
- a day off
- additional annual leave
- additional time during national holidays
- additional time off for maternity or paternity leave
- paid taxis when working overtime or late at night.

The key is to assist staff to strike a balance between workplace requirements and home/life requirements—the elusive "work-life balance". If your practice is successful in this, you will find that highly motivated staff remain with you for the long term.

Management of performance

This section emphasises encouraging management of staff performance. A successful practice has systems in place that allow staff to measure their own performance. Consider the following points:

- Staff must understand what their responsibilities are: What are staff expected to achieve? Where do their responsibilities begin and end?
- Set clear goals for staff to allow them to meet their responsibilities: How will these goals be discussed with the staff? Do staff understand what is to be achieved and believe they can achieve these goals?
- Set clear plans for staff responsibilities: Are staff roles clearly outlined? Are staff responsibilities and job expectations clearly outlined? Are these plans discussed with staff so that they understand what is required and expected of them?
- Discuss the plans and goals for practice success with the staff: Do staff understand what their tasks involve from the point of view of practice success? Do staff understand how their activities fit into the goals for the practice? Do staff understand how important their role is in the success of the practice?
- Establish clear guidelines for performance measurement: Have you discussed with staff how their performance will be measured and what represents success in their performance? Have you been frank in discussing possible barriers that might reduce the quality of their performance and the success of their area of responsibility?

- Establish clear guidelines for performance management: Has there been any discussion on how performance of staff will be measured and evaluated? Have you identified how the failure to meet objectives will be addressed?
- Incentives as a reward for achieving performance should be discussed with staff. Incentives may be financial but there are many alternatives such as access to professional development, promotions, additional time off, a staff dinner, etcetera. A number of small incentives may be more important than one large bonus.
- It is essential that professionals be specific in their requirements and their comments to staff. Vague and general comments are of little assistance in this exercise.

The starting point in performance management is to ensure that each staff member knows exactly what is required of them. For example, a decision may be made to appoint a staff member as a practice patient coordinator. The roles of a coordinator may vary from one practice to the next but could include:

- pre-consultation contact with patients that commences when patients initially contact the practice for an appointment
- arranging appointments at a time appropriate and suitable for the practice and patient
- greeting patients on arrival and preparing them for their consultation
- patient database maintenance and record keeping
- patient recall systems
- follow-up meetings with patients associated with clinical consultation or as means of maintaining contact
- reports on aspects of patient management
- responsibility for the maintenance of a patient lounge
- liaison with all staff regarding practice matters and patient issues that might impact the practice.

This list is merely an illustration of what responsibilities may be associated with this particular position in the practice. Note that the points made in relation to management of performance have to be applied: the role has to be specific, related to setting goals and planning, and staff need to be aware of what is required and how they are expected to perform.

Staff as managers

Staff need to be managers in order to contribute to the success of the practice. Every area of the practice needs to be managed. In fact, each member of staff needs to manage their own responsibilities. By successfully managing their own area, staff contribute to the overall success of the practice. You need to assist staff to become quality managers. The following suggestions can assist in this exercise:

- Ensure that staff you have employed have the ability to manage others even though they may have had little experience in management to date.
- Staff need to understand the goals of the practice and their responsibilities in achieving those goals.
- Staff need to be able to plan their own actions to achieve success in their areas of responsibility. You will be required to advise staff on goal-setting, planning, and measuring performance.
- As managers, attitudes are essential: staff need to have a positive attitude and an approach which is geared towards success. A positive attitude should be one of the bases used when appointing and selecting new staff. Attitudes are important because patients that are in contact with your staff quickly recognise and appreciate a positive attitude. The staff must have positive attitudes towards the healthcare services the practice provides,

the operating systems implemented to assist progress in the practice, the plans established for the future of the practice, support and training of staff, and the ability of the practice to meet the needs of patients.

- It may be necessary to delegate responsibilities in the instance where more than one staff member is appointed to manage a certain area of a practice. Staff members need to understand that not everything can be done by one person: support and delegation from others is essential for success.

- As a manager, staff need to build alliances. This includes linkages with staff within the practice but also with contacts outside the practice who may provide services. There will be alliances with healthcare professionals, government personnel, consultants, etcetera. Such alliances bring positive results for the practice and increase the practice's image.

- As a manager, staff need the ability to communicate effectively. Associated with this communication process is the ability to listen to patients, professionals, support staff, and consultants. The ability to effectively communicate and listen is an important aspect of a practice's image.

- Obtaining feedback on performance and acting on that feedback is critical to the ability of staff to be successful managers. Communication and listening and maintaining a positive attitude are integral to the exercise of obtaining feedback.

- Working in teams is an integral part of encouraging staff to be managers. This aspect is also closely associated with forming alliances, having good communication skills, and being open to feedback. Teams within a practice may involve staff (full-time or part-time) and external consultants.

- Part of being a successful manager is being involved in planning for the future. This involves change and it is important for staff to appreciate that implementing and embracing change is part of their responsibilities and coping with change is essential for practice success.

- As a manager, staff need the ability to be decisive in giving instructions and directions to staff and to be proactive when facing problems and any action to be taken. Professionals have limited time and require specific answers to issues and decisive explanations of action taken.

- As a manager, staff need to set standards which are appropriate for the practice and which are a positive reflection on the practice.

Being positive: bring out the best in your staff

Ideally, the staff employed in your practice would be positive, informative, cooperative, excellent communicators, and have a positive attitude to everyone associated with the practice. Unfortunately, even though great care is taken in selecting and appointing staff, most practices have some staff with negative attitudes and poor communication skills. When hiring new staff, you must be aware of this possibility and consider some strategies to overcome the problem to bring out the best in your staff.

Consider these four types of difficult people:

1. Staff that appear to have no knowledge or understanding of practice activities, are poor communicators, and make little contributions to the practice.

2. Staff that appear to know everything, even though often this knowledge is not relevant to the practice. They do not appear to be interested in changing their views or learning about what is relevant for the practice.

3. Staff that appear to be overly negative to everything and are constantly criticising what might be possible within your practice.

4.   Staff that appear to procrastinate and are incapable of making a decision and taking action—everything is put off until a later time when it may be too late for decisive action.

It is inevitable that at some stage you find yourself with staff that can be categorised into one of the four categories above. The key question is: is it possible to do something about these kinds of employees? To do nothing may be not be in the best interest of your practice. A second possibility is to strongly recommend that those problematic staff members leave the practice so that activities in the practice are not disrupted. A third possibility is to approach these staff members to see if you can change their attitudes and behaviour.

Let's expand upon this third option of trying to change the behaviour of difficult staff members.

Meet with the staff member

The first step is to meet with the staff member and engage your active listening skills. This means to listen carefully and couple that with body language that makes it clear to the staff member you are paying close attention to what they are saying. This may mean varying your facial expression, your hand gestures, your posture, the volume of your responses, and the particular words you might use. If you are dealing with a staff member who does not communicate well, then you need to engage all of your communication resources to encourage them to communicate in some form in order to begin to address their negative attitude. Your listening style and communication methods should suggest to the staff member that you are appreciative and respectful of their opinions and thoughts.

Respond

The second step is to respond to the comments and opinions given by the staff member. Your response has to be in a form that produces a positive reaction. The purpose of this exercise is to change the attitudes and behaviour of the staff member by demonstrating you are sincere and committed to what you say. It is important that your response makes this impression on the staff member if there is to be any behavioural change at all.

Encourage cooperation

The third step is to encourage the staff member to cooperate and to take a positive approach to changing their behaviour and attitude. The last thing you should do is to counter-attack or become negative and defensive. Rather, you must hold your ground, remain firm in your views, and present a strong and decisive case for a change of attitude. Hopefully this encourages the staff member to reconsider their approach to their role in the practice.

This communication process may take some time—it may be that a number of meetings need to be held with the staff member in order to encourage and assist them to change their attitude and behaviour.

Checklist: The importance of staff

Question	Assessment
Consider your predictions of new patients for your practice. How many new staff will you require?	
How would you identify entrepreneurial attitudes of new staff?	
How important is the role of the practice manager in the practice? How can you incorporate this role in your practice if you have not already done so?	
How important is IT expertise in practice staff?	
Do you see a balance between full-time and casual staff within the practice?	
What teams can be used within the practice; for example clinical teams and administrative teams?	
How will you motivate new staff?	

Checklist: Staff recruitment and employment

Question	Answer
Do you have a list of designated positions to be filled by staff appointed in the practice? Does this include the role of a practice manager?	
What are the avenues you can use to source new staff?	
Are you confident in being able to pose questions to potential staff which identify their attitudes towards success in the practice?	
Have you considered the importance of IT in the practice and selecting staff with appropriate IT knowledge? How will you ensure this occurs?	
Have you considered the areas of the practice to be managed by staff and the extent to which staff will provide leadership in each of these areas?	

Question	Answer
What teams can you establish in your practice to help in the development of practice management and practice systems?	
Do you have any thoughts on how you would motivate staff for the benefit of your practice?	
How will you measure the performance of staff and encourage professional development?	
Are you confident in being able to handle difficult situations relating to staff attitudes and behavior?	

Chapter 6: Using Technology Effectively

Why was this chapter written?

It is important to define 'systems' in a healthcare setting. A system can be defined as a procedure, a process, a method, or a course of action designed to achieve a specific result. All businesses need to have in place a set of operating systems to ensure consistency and success. In healthcare practices, practice systems are the building blocks of a successful business. They apply to all areas of the practice and, when effective, the results are consistent, measureable, and benefit the whole practice. These systems are usually included in a practice's policy and procedures manual and this can be the point of reference for how the practice operates. Systems in a healthcare practice can include financial management, administration, patient services, and clinical procedures. These systems address the operation of patient contact, reception duties, administrative and clinical procedures, information management, risk management, accreditation, human resources, and clinical methods.

Each of the 13 subsections in this chapter emphasise the importance of utilising technology to provide high-quality healthcare services. This chapter focuses on the need for effective operating systems—predominantly electronic systems but also some non-electronic systems. We emphasise the importance of professionals and staff being IT literate. We also highlight the fact that there may be a multitude of different operating systems available for the practice and it is necessary for the professional to select those that best meet the needs of the practice. In this regard, you should obtain advice from as many sources as possible—including professional and consulting organisations—to ensure that the best available system is selected and implemented.

The 13 subsections of this chapter include:

1. Why was this chapter written?
2. Technology: patient communications
3. Technology: patient consultation records
4. Technology: patient reports
5. Technology: patient recalls and referrals
6. Technology: financial records and reports
7. Technology: staff record keeping
8. Staff position descriptions and induction programs
9. Protection of computer systems and records
10. Office equipment
11. Office facilities
12. Office and clinical supplies
13. Checklist: Using technology effectively

Technology: patient communications

A feature of all technological systems is the way in which it allows staff to communicate with patients: from the first communication through to the various consultation processes. These systems may involve a number of applications: it should allow staff to contact patients online, via email, via an electronic registration process, or via SMS. The following list represents some specific applications of technology in patient communication:

- Initial contact by patients for their consultation can be undertaken via email, online registration, or SMS.
- Appointments can be made online via the practice website, with email and SMS confirmation systems used to ensure patients are aware of their consultation time and date.
- Personal and clinical information from patients can be recorded electronically by staff (with details supplied via email or personally by patients), entered electronically by patients prior to the consultation, or added electronically by patients via iPad at the practice.
- Personally Controlled Electronic Health Records (PCEHR) are now part of most healthcare practices. This allows for the details of each consultation to be recorded electronically and should include: the date, purpose of the consultation, outcome of the consultation, and any details of prescriptions or referrals. These records can be accessed by all parties involved in patient care, including the patient.
- Patient communications can extend to producing a report for each patient following a consultation. Some sections of the report should be in standardised form with the professional adding specifics for each patient either via dictation or direct entry. This can then be printed out, checked and signed with a copy given to the patient before the patient leaves the practice.
- The practice should have a system of patient follow-up after the consultation. This indicates an interest by the practice for the patient. This should apply even when the consultation process is complete.
- The billing process should be done electronically and this should incorporate electronic health fund claiming where applicable.

- The practice should have a system for regular contact with patients to keep them informed of any changes in the practice and to maintain links with patients. This should include the use of a practice website, Facebook, LinkedIn, and other forms of social media.

Therefore a major application of practice operating systems is the ability to communicate effectively and regularly with patients: before, during, and after the consultation process.

Technology: patient consultation records

During and immediately following each consultation, the professional should prepare and record the outcome of the consultation. A multitude of software programs are available for this purpose: the Medical Industry Software Association has the details of software programs available. Such programs specialise in providing the professional with on-screen options to enter in relevant healthcare information that can arise during the consultation (for example, pathology results, radiology, specialist reports, medications) as well as the ability to include information on recalls, referrals, and any follow-up tests.

When these various programs are evaluated, they need to be reviewed from the perceived needs of your practice at the time and also the needs of your practice into the future. Consider whether any program you implement has the option to be upgraded into the future as your needs change.

An essential element in all software programs is the issue of confidentiality and security of information. Access to patient records needs to be limited; however, if the practice plans to employ staff or external consultants who are involved in patient consultation, then it is necessary for those individuals to have access to patient information. The software program that is used needs to make provision for this kind of access while at the same time maintaining the required level of security over patients' private information. The software program must also allow for staff to make follow-up consultations with patients, referrals, and recalls. Billing procedures and patient financial information and records should be kept separate to these records and should be undertaken by a dedicated staff member.

Technology: patient reports

A final area for comment in this section deals with patient reports as a result of the consultation.

There are two different options to completing these reports. The first option is that reports are completed by a staff member using the software designed to generate patient reports. The details for the data entry are provided by the professional from the notes made during and after the consultation. These notes should be made directly into the software program. The staff member will be able to easily access the personal details for the patient, the reason for the consultation, and the outcome of consultation. This report can be generated while the patient is finalising their bill and making further consultation arrangements. The report should be checked by the consulting professional before being given to the patient.

The second alternative approach is for the professional to complete the patient report using dictating equipment and software. The report can be dictated in the presence of the patient and then an administrative staff member can type the report while the patient waits. The report should be checked by the consulting professional before being given to the patient.

The patient report needs to have the necessary information in it but should be kept as brief as possible, containing comments on the outcomes of the consultation and additional details of prescriptions issued, referrals made, and follow-up consultations agreed to with the patient. Of course, patient reports need to be generated for the referring practitioner and/or any others involved in patient care.

While it might be thought that this approach adds to the costs of each consultation as it slightly extends the consultation, the effort is worth it as it clearly indicates to the patient that the practice is different from others in providing quality services for its patients.

With the introduction of PCEHR (as discussed above), there is a need to understand exactly what should be recorded, how it should be recorded, and who has access. There is information regarding the management of electronic health records and this is available from government bodies, relevant medical associations, and risk advisors. It is important that every practitioner accesses this information.

Technology: patient reminders, follow-up, and referrals

Reminders

Every patient who arranges a consultation should be contacted beforehand by the practice to remind them of the date and time of the consultation. This reduces the rate of "no shows" and is a clear indication to patients that the practice is interested in their business and wishes to ensure that the consultation takes place. This contact should be completed electronically—via email, an online reminder, or via SMS. Electronic reminder systems are essential in reducing staff time and costs as well as providing an excellent service for patients. Where electronic communication is not possible, a telephone call to the patient will suffice. To do this implies that the practice has the required contact details of each patient and how they preferred to be contacted.

Follow-up

Further contact should be made after each consultation to thank the patient for arranging the consultation, remind the patient of the outcome of the consultation, and to ensure that the patient is aware of any procedures to be undertaken as a result of the consultation. This contact could be completed by the patient coordinator with the information obtained from patient reports prepared by the professional following the consultation. The patient report should document any treatment required, any tests required, prescriptions required, recalls where arranged and, where there is no recall required, the report could encourage contact with the practice as a means of maintaining ongoing linkages with patients.

An example of contact with patients via email is set out below:

Dear Mrs X

Thank you for arranging a consultation with our practice today. Here are a few points for you to note as a result of that consultation. First you have a follow-up consultation on Thursday, May 4th at 2.30 p.m. Please make a note of this in your diary. Secondly, you were provided with a prescription for some medication.

Please present this to your pharmacist without delay and follow the instructions for the medication.

Contact this office if you have any questions on what is required.

Sincerely,

Dr Y.

As stated above, all the information required for this email is obtained from the patient report completed by the professional during and following the patient consultation. Copies of all correspondence sent to patients must be kept and filed (preferably electronically) with the patient's other records.

Referrals

Referrals are important for your practice and its patients. Referrals may be arranged for patients to consult with other professionals ("referrals out") and referrals may be received for new patients from other professionals ("referrals in"). There are government requirements that must be complied with in relation to referrals if the patient is being treated using the Medicare system. These requirements—and all of the Medicare compliance requirements—are available on the Medicare website under the heading *Doing Business with Medicare*.[9]

For both types of referrals, the practice needs to have systems in place to document and record these referrals. Please consider the following points:

- Explain to the patient why you are referring them to another professional. Provide sufficient healthcare information on the reason for the referral as well as the specific contact details of the particular professional you are recommending.
- Patients may, in some cases, nominate their own professional for referral purposes. Generally, this is unlikely to be the case since patients do not have the expertise to select the relevant professional for their healthcare needs. Therefore, patients will be relying heavily on your recommendation. However, it may be that you provide two alternatives referrals with a

---

9   See Medicare: http://www.medicareaustralia.gov.au/provider/business/.

brief comment on each and allow the final decision to be made by the patient.

- Part of the referral process is advising the referred professional of the name, relevant background, and clinical reasons for the referral of the patient. This communication should be done via email or online and acknowledgement should be sought from the referred professional so that you are aware that the referral has been received.
- You should expect confirmation of the consultation with the referred professional within a week after it has occurred. If is not the case, then a further email should be sent to the referred professional seeking details of each consultation. This follow-up task can be undertaken by an administrative staff member.
- The referred professional will produce a report for you based on the consultation and this can lead to further communication with the patient regarding action and treatment.

The key point is that referrals out have to be managed effectively—it is an essential part of your professional responsibility to ensure that patients referred to another professional do, in fact, attend that consultation and your practice receives a report from the referred professional as a result of that consultation. Ensuring this happens is a requirement for quality of care for patients.

Technology: financial records and reports

It is important to have effective and efficient operating systems that deal with internal or external accounting and reporting. This subsection deals briefly with the organisation of financial records and reports.

Financial performance figures for the practice must be prepared and be made available for taxation purposes. The Australian

Taxation Office[10] have specific requirements for any business. These are available on the ATO website; however, taxation advice from a professional advisor should always be sought. Taxation compliance requirements make it clear that keeping financial records is not optional. For the success of your business, the financial reports must demonstrate that your practice has:

- covered all expenses
- produced an acceptable level of profit
- ensured that profit level is sufficient to cover the risk involved in owning and operating the practice. This is often referred to as "a return on investment" and should be a figure which is based on hours worked and the qualifications and expertise of the healthcare practitioner.

Financial records and reports also allow you to track the results of your practice on many levels. You can produce reports on income but you can also produce reports on patient demographics, type of consultations, procedures, referrals, and billing trends. As discussed above, reports can give accurate results on the profitability of the practice. They can even give you the information that tells you what it actually costs the practice for a professional to see a patient. Such reports allow you to plan for the future in relation to practice, staffing numbers, and services.

Technology: staff record keeping

Electronic staff records should include the following details:

- hiring details
- job description
- any signed agreement employment documents and contracts

---

10 See the Australian Tax Office: www.ato.gov.au.

- financial records for taxation and superannuation
- performance management records
- long service leave, sick leave, and holiday leave.

Individual staff records need to be kept that contain all relevant personal and employment information, such as that indicated above. These records need to be kept secure and confidential.

One type of staff record relates to costs and expenses and should include the following details:

- salaries
- bonuses or benefits
- allowances for travel, uniforms, meals, and telephone costs
- superannuation and taxation information
- training costs
- payment for membership or subscriptions to professional organisations.

Another type of staff record relates to staff activities and should include the following details:

- responsibilities and duties
- time allocated to patients
- time allocated to other practice activities
- attendance at conferences, seminars, workshops, and other professional development activities
- outcomes of appraisal and performance reviews
- networking activities both internal and external and the outcomes of these activities.

As a result of these reports, you can keep a confidential summary of progress of the staff within your practice which is important for promotion and performance review purposes. As mentioned, these records are confidential and are reviewed only by the individual staff member and the professional.

Staff position descriptions and induction programs

Management of the practice involves accurately and effectively documenting each staff position and its associated responsibilities within the practice. Every position, including fee earners, is documented so there is a clear understanding of what tasks and responsibilities are associated with each position. This needs to occur even though it may be accepted that staff are multi-skilled and prepared to take on various tasks when required.

There is no one format for a position description but the following information is included in most job descriptions in professional practices:

- mission statement for the practice and information on how the mission statement relates to the position
- practice vision, goals, and information on how this relates to the position
- specific objectives or goals related to the position
- accountabilities and tasks which are the major responsibilities of the position
- attitudes required for each task in the position
- detailed daily task list
- specific responsibilities that relate to IT
- work standards associated with the position
- authority held by the person in the position within the practice
- key performance indicators
- skills, knowledge, and competencies expected
- professional development expectations
- general employment conditions
- salary, allowances, and other conditions
- statement on career progression
- statement on measuring performance and achievement with an emphasis on self–assessment

- any specific responsibilities such as patient coordinator, practice nurse, or practice manager.

The position description need not be a lengthy statement but should provide sufficient information to give direction to the staff member employed in the position. These statements should represent the requirements or expectations of you as a professional establishing or owning a practice.

It is also important to have an induction program for new staff members. Such an induction program could include:
- welcome to the practice
- review of the areas of the practice
- meeting all personnel
- explaining workplace requirements and responsibilities
- expanding on the practice mission and vision
- explaining the practice organisation
- review of the practice procedure manual
- training programs and appraisal and promotion requirements
- general administration processes involving telephone, email, online contact, fax, photocopying, mailing, filing
- use of operating software
- emergency procedures
- practice code of conduct
- confidentiality
- ethics
- dress standards
- staff records
- practice facilities
- attitude to patient management
- attitude to patient contact
- accidents in the workplace
- career development within the practice.

Protection of electronic systems and records

Any software program that is used within your practice should be protected with an appropriate security and anti-virus system and firewall protection. If you intend to have wireless hotspot connections in the practice, then you need to have appropriate levels of security in place to ensure that these connections are protected. We recommend engaging an external expert in security and IT-protection software to ensure that your practice is adequately protected. Further protection of practice software can be through an off-site back-up system that ensures all records are safe at all times.

Today many practitioners and practice managers need to access practice information when they are away from the practice and it is important to have such systems in place. For example, General Practitioners visiting patients in hospital or nursing homes and practitioners operating in hospitals are now able to access patient records wherever they are. Similarly, some practices have off-site dictating services to do reports. Such access needs to be protected and special access systems developed.

You also need to decide who has access to patient information and financial performance information. This information is confidential; however, certain staff will be required to have access to it. For example, it may be that clinical staff require access to patient records, the practice manager requires access to financial performance figures, and other professionals (appointed as partners or associates) require access to patient and practice information.

Computer access can be managed so each person in the practice is given access to particular areas of the computer system. For example, reception staff may not have full financial access. They may have to refer any financial adjustments to the practice manager; patient records may only be available to particular clinical staff. The practice manager may be able to access all areas of the system. Computer access is an important risk management strategy in any practice. These should be clearly defined and included in the policy and procedure manual as well as staff records.

Office equipment

It is necessary for us to make the distinction in this chapter between office equipment and office facilities. Office facilities are examined in the subsection below. This subsection examines the equipment required by professionals to provide a high-quality healthcare service for patients.

Office equipment includes items such as:
- facsimile machines
- photocopiers
- printers and scanners
- prescription printers
- laptops for practitioner use outside the practice
- laptops for patient use
- iPads
- phone systems including mobile phones.

This equipment may be required for the short or long term.

You may also need equipment related to the processing of financial information, such as credit card and EFTPOS facilities, software programs to manage patient billing and receipts, and software to store patients' financial records. You need to devise a system whereby patients' clinical records and financial records are stored in such a way that they are easily located by the required staff member but are also kept secure.

We have emphasised the importance of utilising electronic communication in this book but it is also necessary to have a sophisticated telephone system within your practice. Most patients, at least at the initial stage of communication with the practice, are contacted via telephone. There are a range of options out there for commercial telephone systems and the option that you select depends on the precise needs of your practice. Consider purchasing a telephone system that has separate lines, the ability to answer and transfer calls, options for hold music and customised messages, automated operations, intercom systems, paging systems, and voicemail preferences.

Many practices today use their phone system to relay information, such as services offered, times of opening, how to make appointments, and promoting special events or programs; for example, vaccinations.

All purchase of office equipment come with the option of purchase versus lease and these options should be explored to find what best suits your practice.

Office facilities and layout

Office facilities generally refer to the desks, chairs, and computers that make up a practice but contemporary practices are becoming adventurous in supplying facilities for patients. The waiting room can become a patient lounge area. This area is a separate area to the reception area and allows for patients to wait comfortably for their consultation. Avoid the traditional "chairs against the wall" waiting room. The lounge should have facilities such as television, radio, music, computer facilities, hand washing facilities, audiovisual facilities, and refreshment facilities. It should also include paintings, wall coverings, and quality floor coverings. All of these items have a significant impact on the image of the practice to patients.

This patient lounge area can be a source of practice information and education. Many practices now have iPads for patient use, display education programs on a TV, provide healthcare-related reading material, and have facilities set up so that patients can join in relevant networks, such as new parents, the elderly, diabetes support groups, etcetera.

Although the patient lounge is a busy place, there should also be a confidential area for interviews with patients. There are times when staff need to talk to a patient or family away from others. The patient might be upset, they might have received a grim diagnosis, or they might want to discuss a situation they are unhappy about. It is important to have this confidential area as part of your practice.

Care needs to be taken in planning the layout of the practice. Consideration needs to given to planning the purchase and placement of furniture. For example, in the patient lounge it may be that furniture should be arranged in a way which encourages patients to relax prior to their consultation.

The layout and facilities in the practice have a significant impact on the image of the practice to patients. Your image needs to be one of quality to reflect the high standards of your practice and impress patients.

Office and clinical supplies

Office supplies include stationery, cleaning supplies, and general medical supplies. The responsibility for maintaining supplies should be delegated to the practice manager or a dedicated staff member. Generally, stationery supplies are available for regular replenishment from a local stationery office. Make sure you have systems in place to monitor the amount of stationery obtained and used within your practice.

Cleaning supplies can also be obtained from a supplier on a regular basis. Having adequate cleaning supplies are vital for a healthcare practice. These also need to be monitored not only in terms of quantity obtained but also for their safe storage and use.

The amount of general medical supplies needed depends upon the services offered by your practice. A clinical assistant could be responsible for ordering and monitoring these supplies on a regular basis. These supplies could include equipment for the examination of patients, diagnostic equipment, stethoscopes, blood pressure equipment, syringes, sterilisation solutions, covers for beds, and various laboratory investigation supplies. As with office and cleaning supplies, it is important to monitor the amounts ordered and used within the practice.

Checklist: Using technology effectively

Question	Answer
What do you see as a major challenge in ensuring satisfactory communication between your practice and patients?	
Who should maintain patient records–professionals or practice staff?	
How important are patient reminders, recalls, and referrals?	
Should your financial records and reports be prepared internally or should an external professional be employed for this purpose?	
What electronic techniques should be used for communication between staff and between professionals and staff?	
How important is the protection of computer systems and records within your practice?	

Question	Answer
Is phone technology likely to remain important for your practice given the growth in electronic communication?	
Should investment in office facilities be increased in order to create a positive image for patients?	
Can the purchase of office supplies be delegated to staff or should this be retained by each professional?	

Chapter 7: Financial Performance

Why was this chapter written?

The issues in this chapter address financial performance to help you understand what is necessary for your practice to survive and develop. This chapter emphasises key financial concepts, the financial systems required to keep your practice viable, the reports needed to measure progress and performance, the financial advice you may require, the importance of a Board of Advice, and the use of external accountants. All of these issues are significant in deciding on what is to happen with the practice and what needs to be done to keep the practice viable.

The chapter consists of 14 subsections. We begin by discussing your practice as a business and conclude with a personal assessment of your understanding of what is happening in financial terms in your practice. Many users of this book already have some understanding of the issues raised in this chapter. However, it is important to reiterate these issues as they are essential for an understanding of what is important for the practice and its survival.

The 14 subsections of this chapter include:
1. Why was this chapter written?
2. Your practice as a business
3. Financial terms

4. Financial risk
5. Understanding what is required to make your practice viable
6. Financial reports
7. Financial advice
8. Guiding staff to collect and report on finance matters
9. Role of a Board of Advice
10. Role of an external accountant
11. Quality of service and financial performance
12. Use of graphs and charts in measuring financial performance
13. Practice billing and collection of fees
14. Checklist: Financial performance

Your practice as a business

Your practice is a business and, as such, it is vital that you know and understand every aspect of it. Every business—whether these are operations in retail, wholesale, manufacturing, professional practices, or non-profit entities—have revenue sources, long and short-term expenses, and are expected to generate surpluses as profits to ensure they remain financially viable. Thus, every business searches for additional revenue in order to cover expenses.

Profit is not a dirty word; rather, profit is essential for survival. Those setting up a business of any sort must be able to identify the sources of profits and measure profits. For a professional practice, services are provided for patients and this leads to expenses for the practice in terms of staff and associated expenses with the delivery of services. The challenge for the professional practice is to deliver high-quality services while containing expenses and ensuring that revenue exceeds expenses to produce a profit.

In order to ensure that profits are generated, some practices convert their revenue and expenses to "benchmarks" and guidelines. But practice staff may be expected to generate patient fees for services equivalent to (for example, three times) the rates paid to staff. For example, a staff member paid $50,000 may be expected to generate patient fees of at least $150,000. The rationale behind this "three times" standard is: (1) to cover staff salary; (2) to cover expenses; (3) to cover surplus generation. In general, the larger a practice, the higher the benchmark; it is not uncommon for large practices to have benchmark of "seven times".

Whether your practice utilises the benchmark concept or not, it is important for you to understand whether the practice generates sufficient revenue to cover expenses and produce an adequate profit. This "adequate profit" has to cover a reasonable salary for yourself, staff expenses, and operating expenses necessary to deliver services to patients. This is a relationship you need to understand; you need to have some feel for what is a reasonable salary for yourself as a professional in practice and what is adequate revenue to generate surplus to cover salaries of staff and operating expenses in the short and long-term.

Financial terms

Here we list different financial terms and provide an explanation of each with examples where appropriate.

Revenue

In a healthcare practice the revenue generally comes from fees. These can be from consultations, procedures, and other patient services. Other revenue may be generated from a number of sources; for example, government grants and payments, additional healthcare services (such as travel medicine and industrial medicine), and external work such as medico-legal reports and representation on tribunals.

In some healthcare practices–for example, General Practice–some consultation fees are time-based. Consultations fees can be for a standard time or for an extended time where the fee increases accordingly. This is an example of fees based on an hourly rate.

The task of the practice is to increase revenue as much as possible and contain expenses so that the gap between revenue and expenses is sufficient to cover the salary of the professional and general expenses of the practice and produce a profit.

Expenses

This generally represents the amounts paid by the practice in providing services for patients. It is the cost of being in practice and these expenses may include salaries for staff, providing patient services, supporting practice facilities, practice insurance for personnel, buildings, equipment, and registrations. Expenses can be complex; some expenses are met on an annual basis, others are met on a weekly basis. The systems you have in your practice must take care of these different types of expenses. For example, rent for a medical practice may be paid monthly, staff salaries may be paid weekly, expenses such as electricity or gas may be paid monthly or quarterly.

Profit or surplus

Profit or surplus represents the difference between revenue and expenses for a particular period whether it be a week, month, quarter, or a year. The aim of the practice is to ensure that profit or surplus is sufficient to meet and exceed all expenses of the practice, including a salary for the professional. It is easy to say that the aim of the practice is to maximise surplus or profits. It then becomes complicated in the sense that we have to determine what do we mean by "maximising" profits?

Financial risk

There are financial risks with any business and one might argue that one of the financial risks associated with healthcare practices is a reflection of whether patients remain with the practice or move to an alternative practice. Loss of patients may be a relatively high risk. This high risk can be overcome to a certain extent by quality of service and presentation of professionals in providing services. More is said on this in Chapter 3 where we emphasise attracting patients and retaining patients.

Assets

These are items that are owned by the practice and purchased for use in the immediate future and the longer term. Examples include furniture and equipment. These items are needed not only immediately but in future years. Some assets may be purchased for cash whereas other assets may be purchased using credit and paid for over time. A return on assets is important and is seen as essential for long-term survival. What the return on assets should be is a question of debate since it does reflect risk. This leads to the concept of liabilities.

Liabilities

This is the amount owing by the practice to others by way of debt or commitments for services, purchases, or financial obligations such as leases on equipment. Almost without exception, a new healthcare practice utilises funds from a bank to provide for payment of expenses, purchase of assets, and meeting liabilities.

Capital

This represents the difference between assets and liabilities of a practice. For example, a healthcare practice may have purchased furniture and fittings to the total of $40,000 and may have borrowed $10,000 to meet those purchases. Thus, assets total $40,000 and liabilities $10,000, giving a net investment of $30,000. One of the aims of the practice would be to eliminate this debt over time. Capital is a difficult term to understand as it is often used for different purposes. Capital may be used to mean net investment by principals in a practice and this figure is often used when we refer to "return on capital".

In theory, those investing in a healthcare practice would expect to earn a return on the net investment which represents net capital. For example, if a healthcare practice has a net investment of $30,000, the professional may require a return on that of 30 percent or $9,000 per annum plus salary. Healthcare professionals should understand how much they have in the practice by way of net investments and the extent to which a return from revenue and expenses produces a reasonable result on that investment.

Plans

These are projections of practice expectations into the future. Plans generally consist of an estimate of future revenue, future expenses, and future profits.

Targets

These are projected achievements and are often more specific than plans. Targets may represent actual amounts such as profits earned from the use of assets or the use of capital.

Cash flow

This represents the difference between cash received from patients and cash paid for practice expenses. Cash flow must be positive otherwise the practice would not be seen as viable.

Understanding what is required to make your practice viable

In brief, the healthcare professional needs to ensure that fees from patients continue to exceed practice expenses. This is a rather simplistic statement but there are many implications from it:

- The number of patients for the practice should be increased progressively to ensure that total fees exceed total expenses.
- Growth in the range of services is desirable to attract additional patients and additional fees.
- Improvement in the delivery of services is desirable to increase approval rating from patients.
- Quality of contact between healthcare professionals and staff is desirable.
- Control over overall expenses is desirable to increase the gap between revenue and total expenses.
- Some expenses may be deferred to a later financial period. This is necessary to ensure viability of the practice.

In order to achieve the above in one form or another, regular reports on revenue and expenses are essential for the practice with analyses of revenue and expenses to identify potential savings and opportunities to improve performance. In the following section, we provide a potential list of reports that could be a suitable starting point. This is not to suggest that all reports must be prepared by any new healthcare practice but rather that selected reports could highlight areas of potential savings and profit.

Financial reports

All forms of financial reporting are important. By becoming familiar with financial reports, you get to know and understand what can influence or impact your practice financially.

Potential management reports

The following table[11] represents a list of potential management reports that can be generated by specific staff members on a regular basis. This is a suggestion of the type and frequency of reporting that should be used within your practice to ensure that you, as the principal, and all other staff members are kept well-informed about the financial viability and performance of the business.

---

11 Meredith, Geoffrey. *21st Century Medical Practice Management.* Brisbane: Mereton Publishings, 2006. At page 228.

Report	Content	Timing
1. Patient consultations	Daily consultations with clinicians	Daily
2. Referral report	Referral patterns	Monthly
3. New patients	New patients daily and cumulative	Weekly
4. Fees	Fees per clinician, service, nurse, patient type	Daily
5. Patient consultation follow-up	Patients, method, outcome	Daily
6. Patient scheduling	Patient, staff, outcome	Daily
7. Patient treatment cost	Cost of each staff member by service	Weekly
8. Key performance indicators	Various ratios	Monthly
9. Personnel activity summary	Time allocated to patients, administration, training	Quarterly
10. Personnel costs	Costs for each staff member in services for patients	Quarterly
11. Overhead costs	Components of overhead	Monthly
12. Equipment	Operating and maintenance costs	Monthly
13. Cash flow	Cash in/out, balances	Daily/Weekly
14. Profit summary	Fees, expenses, surplus	Monthly
15. Performance, charts, graphs	Cash flow, fees, productivity	Monthly
16. Financial stability	Current and liquidity ratios, break-even points	Monthly
17. Debtor analysis	Money owing and timing	Monthly
18. Practice commitments	Creditors, overdraft, loans	Quarterly
19. Insurance summary	Cover, premiums	Quarterly
20. Plans and control reports	Cash, profits, fees, patients	Monthly
21. Feasibility studies	Proposed expansion	As required
22. Retirement benefits	Superannuation, long service leave	Six monthly
23. Survey feedback	Patients, staff, consultants	Six monthly
24. Promotions	Methods, costs, outcome	Six monthly
25. Services	Service type and patient type	Monthly
26. Board of Advice	Action on key points from meetings	Quarterly

Report	Content	Timing
27. Asset maintenance	Expenditure and assessment	Quarterly
28. Inventory	Type and value	Quarterly
29. Database support	Form, expenditure, outcomes	Quarterly

We are not suggesting that you need all of the reports set out above—part of your duty as a professional is to decide which reports are important and which can be added over time. You also need to decide who prepares the reports—this can be a responsibility of the practice manager or it may be delegated to a particular member of staff—and the timing of the reports, particularly those that occur daily or weekly. For example, report number 1 (Patient consultations) could be prepared by the staff responsible for organising consultations. The same applies to report numbers 2, 3, 4, 5 and 6. Report number 7 may be more complicated as it deals with the cost of each staff member by patient service. With experience, staff should be able to calculate these reports. Report numbers 11 and 12 (Overhead costs and Equipment) may have to be prepared with the assistance of an outside accountant or an employed accountant.

Some of the reports mentioned in the above list arise from specific actions that the practice may or may not decide to take. For example, Report number 21 (Feasibility studies) and 26 (Board of Advice) and others may only arise from efforts initiated within the practice.

Financial advice

The chances of any healthcare professional having all the knowledge necessary to meet the requirements of a healthcare practice are remote. You will continually have to seek advice on non-clinical aspects of your practice; in particular, you need to seek financial and/or legal advice on areas such as:

- development of a financial plan
- communication difficulties
- technical matters associated with compliance
- taxation requirements
- planning and control procedures
- reporting and interpretation of reports
- requirements of professional organisations
- requirements of government (other than normal compliance)
- pricing of services
- practice lease agreements.

This list may be expanded as the practice grows and develops. The issue of seeking advice is connected to identifying and utilising staff members to report on issues of importance. The practice manager can have a key role in the area of financial management of the practice. The role of a Board of Advice may also be relevant in terms of seeking advice. It is important to keep in mind that your aim as a professional healthcare provider should be to allocate as close to 100 percent of your time to the delivery of services for your patients.

Guiding staff to collect and report on finance matters

An important aspect of a healthcare practice is having competent staff that are capable of effectively and efficiently undertaking administrative matters to relieve you, as a healthcare professional, of that task. It is the practice manager who has this as one of their key responsibilities. Depending on their qualifications and experience, you may need to invest in providing training for them with an outside organisation. The extent of this depends upon the degree of financial knowledge of the staff member and their interest in finance matters. In some practices a person is appointed specifically to deal with finance matters, such as an accountant or bookkeeper.

There are considerable advantages to the practice of having confidence in a staff member who can take responsibility for financial reporting and analysis and provide you with vital and relevant information when required. Finance is a critical area in practice management as it relates directly to the sustainability and survival of the practice. A staff member dedicated to finance can ensure that follow-up on certain areas are conducted and can provide accurate and up-to-date financial information when requested. Accuracy in reporting is essential in finance issues; every transaction should be double-checked by a second person. You should also be included in the financial reporting for the practice. Leaving finance matters unchecked is dangerous and can lead to errors in reporting. Part of the operating systems of the practice need to revolve around ensuring that finance matters are continuously checked and double-checked within the practice. The practice of double-checking is not to suggest there is any lack of confidence in staff; it is a recognition that human error can and does happen.

Role of a Board of Advice

The Board of Advice is a group of professionals with expertise, experience, and knowledge in practice management matters who are in a position to give advice on management and planning aspects of your practice. The members of a Board of Advice can include an accountant, lawyer, business consultant, marketing and communications consultant, and IT systems consultant. Members of the Board act as an independent review committee to comment on progress, achievements, and future plans and direction of the practice. Meetings with the Board should be held on a regular basis to discuss key issues concerning the practice, including financial performance. Such meetings need to be tightly controlled and monitored, with a comprehensive agenda distributed prior to the meeting and minutes circulated after the meeting.

Principals and staff of the practice should be aware that the Board will be invited to see financial performance figures from the practice and will:

- review progress in achieving objectives and goals of the practice
- review financial performance over specific periods
- review proposed future plans.

It is imperative that staff listen and consider any advice, recommendations, or comments of the Board. The Board is regarded as an advisory body only; it has no ultimate authority over the practice or responsibilities in terms of decision-making. The decisions in the practice are yours.

Members of the Board are to be trusted, respected, and seen as appropriate counsellors or consultants in advising you and your staff on the direction of your practice. Board members need to be good communicators and have the ability to provide advice and recommendations. Members may, from time to time, act as mentors to staff.

Payments to members of the Board should be agreed to—they are giving up time to assist your practice and they should be financially rewarded. This means that you, as the professional, need to be satisfied that the decisions of the Board are worth the financial costs to a practice for their time and efforts.

Selection of members of the Board depends upon, to some extent, the degree of involvement you require from the Board. For example, if the primary focus of the practice initially is contact with patients and involvement of patients in the practice, then you may select members of a Board who can best advise you on that.

Role of an external accountant

Most, if not all, healthcare practices utilise the expertise of a firm of accountants, at least for the preparation and submission of annual taxation returns and other taxation matters. For these matters, the accountants act as an independent reviewer of performance of the practice in reporting to government on revenue, expenses, and profits of the practice.

In addition to advice on taxation matters, there are advantages in selecting an accountant to advise the practice on financial operating systems. When you set up your practice, an accounting firm should be able to advise you on what systems to introduce to guarantee efficiency and effectiveness in financial performance. You may also be able to obtain advice on the financial performance of the practice—the accountant may be able to pass judgement on the efficiency of your practice's financial operating systems and make recommendations of changes to be introduced. For these reasons, it is important that you select the external accountant carefully. In the long term, it may be that your practice seeks the services of not one but two external accountants: one firm to provide expertise and service in taxation matters and the second to advise on financial performance. These are issues that can be discussed and reviewed over time.

Quality of service and financial performance

Quality of service is the centre of a healthcare practice. Patients will be attracted to your practice if you can demonstrate ongoing and effective quality in the services you provide. Evidence of quality control is often demonstrated through practice accreditation. To obtain accreditation, practices provide the approved organisation with details of operating systems, procedures, policies, and records as well as practice compliance in specific areas. A separate organisation in Australia has been set up to assess practices in terms of the quality and standard of the services provided. Practices are then awarded accreditation by an accrediting organisation; for example, AGPAL (Australian General Practice Accreditation Ltd), QIP (Quality Innovation Performance) or GPA Accreditation Plus. Practices often display evidence of accreditation (usually by way of certificate) in the practice to provide reassurance as to the high standard of services provided to its patients.

Quality of service from a practice can be evaluated in a number of different ways, such as:

- the ability of your practice to deliver prompt and effective services
- accessibility of services
- reliability, consistency, credibility, and dependability of services
- ability of personnel to communicate with patients and follow patient requirements
- respect for privacy
- the physical appearance of the practice.

In this regard, the core values of any practice are important in setting the tone and direction of the practice and establishing attitudes and approaches to patients. The core values of a practice are those values which form the basis of how the practice functions and how everyone in the practice behaves.

Having a strong set of core values underpins the whole practice and should become part of the induction for each individual working in the practice. It can be one of the main reasons for the recommendation of a practice by a patient to others. Keep in mind that we wish to recruit patients who will act as ambassadors for a practice. Hence, the quality of practice services and core values are important.

Measuring financial performance

There are significant advantages in presenting financial performance information in a visual format using charts or graphs. These often show useful relationships between various factors that influence practice performance.

As an exercise, we suggest that you review the 29 reports listed above and identify 10 reports that you might use. Comment on the relationships demonstrated by these reports and whether charts or graphs could be produced to show these relationships. For example, Report 1 could show the relationship between the number of patients and the total minutes or hours of consultations with clinicians; Report 2 could demonstrate the changing number of new patients every day; and Report 12 could show the relationship between cash received and cash paid and cash balances every day or every week.

We commend the use of charts and graphs for your practice as they produce useful information for your decision-making.

Practice billing and collection of fees due

It is self-evident that for a practice to be viable fees must be billed and collected. The Australian Government has a Schedule of Fees that is produced annually and some healthcare organisations—for example, the AMA—produce a list of fees for patients. However, the final decision on what is charged for services is up to the professional. In general practice, fees are often based on the length of time of the consultation with provision for extended consultations, procedures, tests, out-of-hours consultations, and home visits. Specialists in healthcare tend to bill patients based on the consultation format—the initial consultation, follow-up consultation, tests or procedures.

In the case of financial hardship by a patient, the healthcare professional has the ability to waive fees or substantially reduce fees should they decide to do so. Overall, the healthcare professional has to balance such decisions against the need to produce fees for the practice.

The method of collection of fees has changed over time. At present, there is a tendency to collect fees at the time of the consultation so that there are no fees owing to the practice at any given time. Where there is a system of billing in terms of accounts, the practice will have debtors which represent an asset or money due to the practice; however, if the level of debt is exceedingly high, this may cause financial difficulties for the practice, hence the tendency to collect fees at the time of consultation.

What is important is that every practice should have a billing policy in place so that all patients are aware of any fees and there is agreement on how and when those fees will be paid. There are responsibilities regarding informed financial consent for patients where there is a cost to the patient. Having a clear understanding of practice billing is in the patient's interest as well as the interests of the practice

In an ideal world, a new practice will have a continuous flow of patients who are prepared to pay for consultations at the time. It is highly likely that patients will pay for consultations using a credit card; however, these can be converted quickly to the equivalent of cash for the practice.

Checklist: Financial performance

Question	Assessment
Do you agree that understanding financial matters is critical to understanding the viability of the practice?	
Do you regard the practice as a business?	
What is your approach to cash receipts, cash payments, and fees on a short-term and long-term basis?	
Are there any terms in this chapter which you need to gain more information about?	
Of the 29 reports listed in the table, which 10 do you see as being most important for the long-term viability of your practice?	
Which of the reports are you not familiar with? Do you believe that you should learn more about the preparation and production of such reports?	

Question	Assessment
Are there areas of financial matters which you need assistance in gaining a greater understanding? Where can you seek advice to help you with this?	
Will you include financial management as part of the role of the practice manager?	
Do you think it is possible to hire staff who can assist you in finance matters? Are you happy to provide additional training for such staff?	
Do you see a role for a Board of Advice for your practice? Can you think of four professionals who may act as members of your Board of Advice?	
Would there be a conflict between a Board of Advice and external accountants hired to assist or advise your practice?	
Can you see the benefit in converting your information on finance matters to charts and graphs?	

Chapter 8: Financial Planning

Why was this chapter written?

A vital aspect of starting into practice involves planning. What do we mean by "planning"? Planning is about setting goals for you and your practice and then developing the strategies and detailing the tasks involved in achieving these goals. You can have overall business plans, operational plans, practice development plans—basically, you are planning the life cycle of your practice! In this section we discuss one of the most basic and most important areas of planning for your practice: financial planning.

This chapter is divided into 12 subsections that focus on the need for effective financial planning and include:

1. Why was this chapter written?
2. Planning is not an optional extra
3. Financial expenses and overheads
4. Understanding practice profit
5. What clinicians need to know
6. Focusing on key areas: patients, fees, and cash
7. Converting cash to profit estimates
8. Planning: the role of staff
9. Planning: Board of Advice
10. Compiling a comprehensive practice plan
11. Converting patients to practice ambassadors
12. Checklist: Financial planning.

Planning is not an optional extra

Many professionals who are interested in establishing their own healthcare practice do not regard planning as an essential component of their practice set-up. Planning is seen as something that is "desirable" but not "essential". This is a mistake. Planning should be an automatic part of any establishment. Planning answers a host of questions for any potential owner, such as the following:

- What is likely to happen in the upcoming months in the practice?
- Will fees exceed expenses?
- What are the costs for insurance, risk, and compliance?
- What growth prospects exist?
- What key decisions need to be made?
- What barriers will be faced?
- Is extra effort needed to bring in new patients and generate additional fees to cover expenses?
- What are the practice establishment costs?
- What are the costs of equipment?
- How will we fund these costs: lease, purchase, rent?
- What additional expenses are expected in the coming year?

You need to allocate time for the planning process of the practice, regardless of whether you are establishing a new practice or joining an existing practice. The ability to plan and to manage your time as a professional is an essential part of building a viable practice. Each week time should be set aside for practice planning. Decisions need to be made as to what plans are essential for the practice and how these plans can be prepared, documented, and cross-checked. If necessary, obtain assistance from experienced external consultants to prepare these plans. Remember, planning is an essential—not an optional—element of the success of your practice.

Financial expenses and overheads

Financial record keeping can be complex. For a new or established practice wishing to expand, it is important to:
- ensure that operating systems are relatively simple
- arrange matters so that staff can maintain basic financial records
- ensure that the information available is adequate for taxation and compliance purposes
- ensure that operating systems are designed to monitor your practice's viability and growth.

In order to have effective internal operating systems for financial planning, you need to understand what financial matters are significant for your practice. These financial matters can be categorised into two groups:
- day-to-day financial expenses as a result of operations within the practice
- practice overheads which are necessary to establish the practice and are essential for long-term practice development.

Examples of day-to-day expenses include staff wages, communication expenses (such as telephone, internet, fax), stationery, medical equipment, advertising or promotions, interest charges, insurance, payments for consultants, practice rates, and utilities. All of these items can be identified with regular invoices from suppliers or the equivalent. Your practice needs to have a system where these invoices are collated and reported on regularly.

Practice overheads can be divided into two groups:
- overheads associated with patient services which may include clinical material, specific equipment, staff salaries, and allowances associated with providing services
- overheads associated with operations which may include salaries and wages (other than those included in the

practice daily expenses account), insurance, repairs and maintenance of practice facilities, costs associated with equipment, expenses associated with communications, lease and rental payments, costs associated with furniture and equipment, and refurbishment of your practice.

To repeat a point made in earlier in this book: it is important to recognise that the total revenue from patient fees must exceed the total expenses of operating the practice. One of the bases for measuring performance is balancing the fees from patients and practice expenses. Financial complications tend to arise because fees are usually received daily or weekly, while a majority of practice expenses are spread over weeks or months. The key is to match your expenses with your revenue. For large practices, this is a task for a qualified accountant who may be employed within the practice or may be engaged externally.

Here are some simple examples:

- Compare fees in one month to fees in a previous month to establish growth in fees: if fees this month were $30,000 and fees last month $28,000, this represents a growth in fees of just over 7 percent.
- Dealing with expenses is more complex as expenses can occur daily, weekly, monthly, quarterly, or biannually. However, where fees can be converted to the equivalent of expenses per week, an estimate of profit can be made: if patient fees this week were $11,600, and the cost of practice operations this week is $6,800, this indicates a surplus for the week of $4,800.

Patients want to be associated with a financially viable practice and they recognise this viability by observing the environment of the practice, staff and their presentation, and the general attitudes of those associated with the practice.

Consequently, on all issues relating to finance, there is merit in obtaining professional advice from an accountant.

Understanding practice profit

This section examines how your practice can plan for producing and maintaining a profit to ensure that your practice remains viable from the time of establishment. Overall, the practice revenue needs to cover all expenses plus overheads. Any practice should engage professional financial assistance to identify how to measure expenses and compare them with revenue to ensure the practice produces a profit.

Profits can be increased by any combination of the following:
- increasing the number of patients serviced by your practice
- increasing the fees per patient
- reducing practice expenses.

The key to this is to ensure that the practice is financially viable; that is, with a sufficient level of profit to justify its continuation and satisfy the needs of its owner(s). In general, there are two components of profit requirements for any practice owner:
- a salary: an amount necessary to allow a practice owner to meet the daily costs of living while meeting the requirements of being a professional in practice
- a return on investment: unless the practice produces a return on investment, the practice will not be financially viable.

For example, you (as a healthcare professional) may determine that a weekly salary of $2,000 is required in order for you to meet the costs of operating a new practice. You may also have an investment in the practice of $50,000 and believe that a return of 10 percent is justified (representing an additional $5,000 per annum). Based on these figures, you can calculate the amount of money required to justify the long-term viability of the practice. These calculations are directly related to the financial information available to you. This is examined further in the following section.

What clinicians need to know

In brief, the owners of a healthcare practice need to understand that your practice is an investment. Your practice has a value. To be on top of the operational side of your practice, you need to have details relating to:

- the financial viability of the practice in the short term
- the long-term survival of the practice in financial terms
- the potential growth of the practice over time
- what it costs to see a patient.

On a daily basis, owners of a practice need financial information which demonstrates the total amount of patient fees each day and the expenses related to the tasks of treatment and consultation. This information can be supplied by practice support staff who register patients and have details of the specific practice expenses.

Example: Simplified annual performance statement

Fees	$350 000
- Total salaries	$225 000
- Overheads	$105 000
= Surplus	$ 20 000

In terms of the long-term survival of the practice, assume that a sole practitioner operating a new practice expects patient fees of $350,000, total salaries for clinical and non-clinical staff to be $225,000, and overheads of $105,000. As set out in the statement above, this leaves a surplus of $20,000 for the year.

An indication of long-term profitability can be obtained by converting that performance statement into a statement indicating the cost of each consultation and the likely profit from each consultation. Based on the above statement, the overhead mark-up rate is calculated based on the fact that overheads are $105,000 and total salaries are $225,000. This means for every $1 of staff salary, 47 cents in overheads are expected ($105,000/ $225,000) or the equivalent of 47 percent of salaries. Use this calculation to add an overhead allowance for consultation services provided to patients. If the salary component of a consultation is (say) $21.55, we can extend this by 47 percent, which is $10.13. This means that the total estimate of the consultation is $31.68. Assuming the fee for the consultation is $50.00, we then know there would be a surplus from this consultation of $18.32.

If, on the other hand, the new practice charged $35.00 as a fee for the consultation, then the surplus would be reduced to $3.32. If the consultation had been charged at $30.00 per patient, it means that this practice would be losing funds for each consultation.

Patient fees may be set based on the government schedule of fees (Medicare) or recommendations of a professional body—for example, the AMA or calculated by the professional operating the practice. Whatever method is used, it is important to be aware of the connection between practice costs and fees so that you understand whether a profit or a loss is being made on each consultation.

Focusing on key issues: patients, fees, and cash

Patients

Any professional responsible for a practice requires information on fees, patients, and cash—all are important for the short-term survival of the practice. Often, this information may be presented in graph form rather than numbers.

A major weakness of many healthcare practices is a failure to provide professionals with adequate information about the background of each patient. Traditionally, new patient information is restricted to such mechanical items as:

- name, address, and phone number
- date of birth
- key identification details for pensions, Medicare, or private health insurance.

In order to be able to treat patients in totality, much more information should be obtained and provided to healthcare professionals, such as:

- personal relationships
- details of family life
- employment type and commitments
- languages spoken
- whether patients are Australian citizens or not
- friends or other relatives living in the home
- any special needs of the patient.

This type of information allows the professional to assess the total care needs of the patient and to act accordingly.

Fees

Graphs can be prepared for patient numbers on a monthly basis that compare actual and target fees. This provides the professional with information on trends and patterns in fee-setting.

Cash

It is necessary for staff to provide a simple five-line statement on cash available on a daily basis: the cash balance at the beginning of the day, cash banked each day, withdrawals from the bank either as cheques or other withdrawals, and a balance at the end of the day. This could be compared to plan versus actual as a trend in cash control.

Example: Cash Performance

	Plan (as at yesterday)	Actual (as at today)	Difference	Explanation
Available 8.00am	$17,360	$17,360		
Cash banked today	$8,700	$9,840	+$ 1,140	Cheque from government
Cash available	$26,060	$27,200	+$1,140	
Cheques written	-$11,400	-$12,600	-$1,200	Extra drawings
Available 6.00pm	-$14,660	$14,600	-$60	
Actual bank balance: $15,440.				

In the above example, note that any difference between the cash balance at the end of a day and the actual cash balance is explained through cheques not being presented or deposits not being recorded by the bank. The figures recorded within a practice is the most accurate and relevant for professionals.

Converting cash to profit estimates

A key to the success of a practice is the knowledge of the costs of each consultation and the surplus from those consultations based on the fees charged. This information is linked to what has been discussed above in terms of profit statements and profit per service for each patient.

We now illustrate how these calculations can be made, taking a hypothetical example of a practice with one doctor, one registered nurse, a practice manager, and one staff member. Please note this is an example for the purposes of providing calculations only.

Example

Personnel	Weekly salary	Hours with Patients	Cost/hour	Cost/minute
Doctor	$2,000	30	67	1.12
Registered nurse	$1,000	30	33	0.55
Practice manager	$1,000	20	50	0.83
Office staff	$500	30	17	0.30

This table provides details of anticipated weekly salaries, hours per week with patients, and the cost per hour and per minute. Figures showing costs per minute are important as the majority of consultations may be 10 minutes or less and the costs of these consultations are equally as important as a consultation or service which may last for one hour or longer.

Example: Service A

Personnel	Time with patient	Cost per consultation
Doctor	10 minutes	11.20
Registered nurse	8 minutes	4.40

Practice manager	5 minutes	4.15
Office staff	6 minutes	1.80
Total		**21.55**

As can be seen from the table above, the cost per minute for the doctor is $1.12 ($11.20/10). This reduces to 30 cents for the office staff member. The cost will obviously be based on a weekly salary of the staff member concerned and the number of hours each staff member has with patients. This information can be used to calculate the labour costs of each consultation.

The cost will depend upon the number of minutes each staff member has with patients. In this example, the total number is 29 minutes and the total cost in terms of labour is $21.55. This can be adjusted (as shown above) to incorporate overheads and provide a total estimated cost of the consultation. This can then be compared with fees to indicate a surplus (or lack of surplus as the case may be). This is an important exercise in establishing the short and long-term financial viability of any practice. There is no point in staff increasing the time with each patient if this time, when costed, results in the practice losing money on each consultation.

Planning: the role of staff

Earlier in this book, we emphasised that staff are part of the key assets of a practice. It also needs to be recognised that planning for a practice depends on the attitudes and expertise of the staff. Consider the impact that staff have on your practice in the following:

* communication with patients

- communication with other healthcare professionals, suppliers, hospitals, government (Medicare, DVA), health funds
- costs of office materials and equipment
- time associated with registering, recording, interviewing, and preparing patients for consultations
- appointment scheduling
- practice billing.

There is no question that effective and efficient staff are essential for a practice to operate successfully without wasted resources or wasted time. This reinforces the point made in earlier chapters that the training of staff is essential for the future of any practice.

We have included appointment scheduling as part of the role of staff in financial planning. It is so important to understand that how patients are booked for appointments can have a direct impact on practice income. For example, if all appointments are for existing patients having a follow-up consultation or short consultations, the income for the day drops. If appointment scheduling is planned and there is a mix of appointment types and procedures, this also affects daily income. Such planning of how you want to book appointments allows you to include appointments for emergencies, Telehealth, home visits and will make a difference to practice productivity.

Patient billing is a system that needs to be planned and understood by practitioners, staff, and patients. Everyone needs to know the billing policy of the practice: how are fees set? When do you expect patients to pay for services? Do staff know how to comfortably and professionally discuss payment with patients? By this, we mean that staff need to be proficiently trained to discuss fees with patients before they come for an appointment or in relation to any treatment or procedure that might be recommended. This investment in educating staff to talk about fees is a positive exercise for the patient and the practice. In fact, informed financial consent is compulsory if the patient is using a private health fund as payment.[12]

Planning: Board of Advice

Professional advice has to be a foundation of starting into practice and throughout the journey of being in practice. We have previously mentioned the notion of a practice obtaining advice from external professionals (from the healthcare industry or otherwise) specifically selected to assist in planning, strategy development, control, and guidance by way of a Board of Advice.

The Board of Advice provides an alternative to engaging individual professionals to consult to the practice. Members of a Board of Advice could include the accountant, a lawyer, a practice development consultant, a marketing consultant, an IT specialist, and a financial planner.

In this context, we discuss planning in terms of putting in place plans for the practice and control in terms of how we actually set the standards, look back, measure, compare and evaluate the results of what the practice has achieved.

From the point of view of planning and control, the Board provides advice on:
- the general strategy in setting up the practice plan and control system
- the starting point in preparing plans or the development of new plans if the practice has already commenced a process of planning and control

---

12 See the Australian Medical Association's publication *Let's Talk About Fees*: https://ama.com.au/ausmed/informed-financial-consent-1

- staff who are responsible for planning processes and procedures to be followed in establishing strategies and converting these to formal plans and budgets
- incorporating plans and budgets into reporting
- the use and format of software reports
- the frequency and format of report presentation
- the interpretation of reports
- the use of visuals for reporting plans and reporting on performance
- assisting in gathering and evaluating data for planning processes.

As a result of this, for every Board of Advice meeting there are two items to be discussed:

- actual performance data compared against plans prepared and approved and an explanation of the differences between expectations and actual performance
- review of plans prepared for the future.

The use of a Board of Advice is an effective method of implementing plans for a new or expanding practice.

Compiling a comprehensive practice plan

A starting point in any practice plan is to document exactly what your practice should be achieving: what do you want from your practice over time? The following eight points provide you with a starting point of what issues to consider in a practice plan—the first seven culminate in number eight, which is image creation and development:

- patient satisfaction as a measure of meeting patient needs
- quality control throughout every aspect of the practice
- financial stability and success

- innovation: being "different" in meeting the healthcare needs of the community
- performance and productivity of staff
- workplace environment and the extent to which it is positive, motivational, encouraging, and entrepreneurial
- the growth and development of all staff (full-time, part-time, external, or internal)
- the practice image and the building and maintenance of that image at the highest possible level.

Now consider the business development aspect of your practice plan. The following points provide you with some issues to include:

- The first activity of any business plan is a clear statement of the practice vision: what the practice is about and what it hopes to achieve over time.
- Provide details of the practice strategies, goals, intentions, and expectations that are designed to deliver the highest quality of healthcare services for patients.
- Outline a series of plans to coordinate these strategies and provide information to be used for decision-making; for example, plans concerning patients, services, finance, networking, marketing, and promotions.
- Provide details of control mechanisms that can monitor many aspects of your practice: what reports are appropriate? What is the format of these reports? Compare actual performance against planned performance and have strategies to correct anything which appears to be out of line with the approved plans.

With this general information in mind, a comprehensive practice plan should have information set out in five sections:

- plans for patients, services, patient mix, and service mix
- staff plans for internal and external staff

- networking, marketing, and promotion plans
- financial and operating plans
- strategic plans; for example, refurbishment plans or restructuring plans.

Converting patients to practice ambassadors

This book discusses the barriers that may lead to dissatisfaction amongst patients. These barriers include difficulty in obtaining consultations, excessive waiting time, and lack of information on procedures and outcomes of consultations. Not all of your patients will take issue with these barriers. Patients may fall into one of three groups:

- patients who are generally satisfied with the consultation process without being overly enthusiastic and recommending the practice to others
- patients who are actively opposed to the practice. This group will not assist the practice and every effort should be made to avoid producing such patients
- patients who are satisfied with the practice to the extent they recommend the practice to others. This group of patients are often referred to as "practice ambassadors".

A long-term aim of any practice is to develop practice ambassadors as these patients are a means to attract new patients to the practice. To achieve this, every staff member needs to be aware of the conditions that lead to the development of practice ambassadors. This aim should be continuously built into the attitudes of staff and the long-term strategies for staff development. Practice ambassadors can bring financial benefit to the practice by encouraging them to promote the practice.

Checklist: Financial planning

Question	Answer
Is financial planning currently an essential part of practice development? If not, what can be done to improve this?	
What do you think is the starting point in financial planning? We suggest that you start with internal records and internal systems. If your method is different, is it working or could it be improved?	
What is your current arrangement on financial planning for practice expenses and overheads and how can this be improved?	
What is the most effective way to plan and develop practice profit and profit estimates?	
Do you accept that financial planning and development has to be undertaken by external professionals while other aspects can be controlled and operated internally?	

Question	Answer
What financial information do you require when planning a new or expanded healthcare practice?	
What financial plans are required to focus on patients, fees, and cash?	
How important are staff in controlling practice expenses?	

Chapter 9: Compliance and Risk Management

Why was this chapter written?

Compliance is an area of running a practice that you cannot ignore. Meeting compliance requirements is not optional for professionals in any practice—a breach of requirements has legal implications and a negative impact on the reputation of your practice in the community. This chapter examines what compliance means for a practice and the various compliance requirements that apply based on the business structure, practice type, professionals and staff, practice services, the process for managing risk, use of information technology, and corporate governance of the practice. In addition, this chapter suggests management procedures for compliance, including the preparation and use of a compliance register and the actions that might follow.

The 15 subsections of this chapter include:
1. Why was this chapter written?
2. Australian Standards
3. The impact of compliance requirements
4. Compliance requirements: practice organisation and type
5. Compliance requirements: personnel
6. Compliance requirements: risk management
7. Compliance requirements: insurance
8. Compliance requirements: patient services
9. Compliance requirements: communicating with patients

10. Compliance requirements: patient complaints
11. Compliance requirements: information technology
12. Compliance requirements: governance
13. Compliance requirements: compliance management programs
14. Practice action for compliance breaches
15. Checklist: Compliance requirements

Australian Standards

In Australia, Standards Australia[13] apply to all businesses and industries. There are particular Standards that apply to healthcare and to practice management; for example, compliance programs, risk management, and records management. Understanding the relevant Standards helps practices identify the compliance requirements for their practice.

What is a Standard?

Standards are published documents setting out specifications and procedures designed to ensure products, services, and systems are safe, reliable, and consistently perform the way they were intended to. They establish a common language which defines quality and safety criteria.

Standards can be guidance documents and include:
• Australian Standards®
• International Standards and Joint Standards
• Codes
• Specifications
• Handbooks
• Guidelines.

---

13 See Standards Australia: www.standards.org.au.

These documents are practical and are not designed to set impossible goals. They are based on sound industrial, scientific, and consumer experience and are constantly reviewed to ensure they keep pace with new technologies. The documents cover everything from consumer products and services, construction, engineering, business, information technology, and human services to energy and water utilities, the environment and much more.

Definition of compliance

Compliance is an outcome of an organisation meeting its obligations. Policies and procedures to achieve compliance must be integrated into all aspects of how the organisation operates. Compliance should be aligned to the overall strategic objectives. An effective compliance program will support these objectives.

Compliance should, while maintaining its independence, be integrated with the organisation's financial, risk quality, environmental and health and safety management systems and its operational requirements and procedures.

A simpler definition from the Australasian Compliance Institute Quick Guide ACI 2008 is:

> *Compliance is the process by which organisations identify and meet strategic obligations whether arising in law, standards and codes of conduct or from stakeholder expectations.*[14]

---

14 See Australian Compliance Institute: www.acigrc.com.

The impact of compliance requirements

Compliance programs for a practice have a significant impact on patient satisfaction and value and ultimately on the success of the practice.

A compliance program aims to:

- ensure the practice meets all compliance requirements of government, community, and professional organisations. These can include legislation, regulations, codes of conduct, membership of professional organisations; for example, colleges and associations, continuing professional development, registrations, and licences
- prevent, identify, and correct any breaches of compliance
- produce training programs to ensure staff and professionals are aware of compliance requirements
- encourage staff to report breaches of compliance requirements
- seek to improve compliance procedures and create a compliance-aware culture.

The sources of compliance requirements that may have an impact on your practice could include any or all of the following:

- State or federal legislation: for example, the *Corporations Act 2001* (Cth), the various *Taxation Administration Acts*, the *Privacy Act 1988* (Cth), the Electronic Transactions Act 1999 (Cth), the various Consumer Credit Codes, and the *Fair Work Act 2009* (Cth)
- licenses and regulations at state and federal or local government levels
- regulatory bodies and professional associations such as medical boards, professional groups, medical defence organisations, accrediting organisations, and professional advisors.

The Australian Standard on Compliance Programs[15] defines compliance as:

> *Compliance is an outcome of an organisation meeting its obligations. Policies and procedures to achieve compliance must be integrated into all aspects of how the organisation operates. Compliance should be aligned with the organisation's overall strategic objective. An effective compliance program will support these objectives. Compliance should, while maintaining its independence, be integrated with the organisation's financial, risk, quality, environmental, and health and safety management systems, and its operational procedures. An effective organisation-wide compliance program will result in an organisation being able to demonstrate its commitment to compliance with relevant laws, including legislative requirements, industry codes, organisational standards, as well as standards of good corporate governance, ethics and community expectations.*

Compliance requirements: practice organisation and type

A management program to meet compliance requirements builds a protective barrier against risk. A combination of a culture of compliance with adequate risk management plans allows a practice to comply with its legal and ethical obligations. The structure, location, and services offered by your practice impacts on the compliance requirements you are obliged to meet.

The compliance requirements related to the structure of your practice could include:

---

15 See *AS3806:2006: Compliance Programs*: www.standards.org.au

- requirements of the Australian Taxation Office through the *Taxation Administration Act 1953* and other key pieces of legislation
- business registration and licenses, particularly those associated with specialised medical equipment
- copyright issues such as patents and trademarks associated with activities of the practice
- insurance requirements associated with buildings, employees, contents, and professional liability
- collection and storage of patient information
- privacy and confidentiality of patient information
- informed consent requirements of patients for medical procedures
- billing requirements for Medicare, health funds or Workcover
- communicating outcomes of consultations to patients
- staff issues: human resources, staff management, WHS, IR, record keeping, privacy.

The registration and licensing requirements associated with medical equipment and specialised procedures depends on the type of practice that you operate and the services that you offer. Some equipment must be licensed or registered to be able to be used in a healthcare practice. Some equipment may only be used by practitioners with specific registration. For example, if a practice wishes to conduct specialist surgery, they are required to comply with various requirements, licenses, and accreditation. This applies to practitioners with specialist qualifications and practices such as surgeons, dentists, pathologists, etcetera. Practice accreditation now applies to most areas of healthcare practice and this includes compliance with set standards across all areas of practice. Professional Colleges and Associations have particular regulatory requirements and these can include codes of conduct and continuing professional development and these must be met in order to continue operating as a healthcare practice.

Medicare and health fund compliance impacts on billing procedures and the method used to convey information to patients; for example, patient consent and informed financial consent, arrangements with patients on procedures, and the application of the *Privacy Act 1988* which applies to all organisations that obtain personal information of individuals.

Issues relating to privacy and confidentiality of discussions between patients and professionals are becoming increasingly important. Adequate privacy measures means that a practice needs to have effective and efficient operating systems, practice manuals, and vigorous staff training and appraisals that clearly define staff's obligations and responsibilities.

Sections of the *Competition and Consumer Act 2010* (Cth) are applicable in terms of disclosure to patients of any financial or other interest (ownership of day surgeries, hospitals), advertising, promotions, and patient fees.

Compliance requirements: personnel

The term "personnel" includes the professionals operating your practice, any allied staff associated with practice activities, support staff who have various roles in the practice, and those external to the practice who provide services (such as members of a Board of Advice, accountants, or IT consultants). Compliance requirements for personnel are related to the services offered by the practice.

Compliance requirements for personnel include:
- various codes of conduct for healthcare services offered in the practice—this can include the college or association, hospital or practice codes of conduct

- various codes of conduct for different roles of professionals and staff—each area of the practice may have particular codes of conduct; for example, practice manager, practice nurse, allied health staff
- registration of professionals with medical boards, medical colleges, professional associations, hospitals, Medicare, and health funds
- registration of registered nurses and allied health professionals applies in the same way as practitioners
- professional development and training requirements of professionals and staff and the recording of this within the practice. In some instances this can be a requirement of practice accreditation or professional colleges and associations
- compliance requirements associated with referrals of patients to the practice and referrals to other healthcare practices.

In addition, there are legislative requirements for practice personnel to comply with the *Fair Work Act 2009* (Cth). This legislation—which covers the national workplace relations system—applies to the majority of workplaces in Australia. It is important to be aware of, understand, and be guided by professional advice regarding this legislation. The Fair Work Commission ensures "employers and employees in the national system all have the same rights and obligations, regardless of which state they work in".[16]

Some of these requirements can apply to all personnel and include:[17]

- employment conditions and standards as set out in the *Fair Work Act 2009* (Cth)

---

16 See Fair Work Commission: www.fwc.gov.au/creating-fair-workplaces.
17 See Fair Work Commission: www.fwc.gov.au.

- levels of wages and salaries for particular positions
- recruitment procedures
- workplace operations
- workplace health and safety
- discrimination and complaints-handling
- insurance
- performance appraisals and reviews
- privacy and confidentiality policies.

Compliance requirements: risk management

Every enterprise, including healthcare practices, operate under conditions of risk. In the majority of cases, it is impossible for any professional to completely eliminate risks; what can be done is to identify, control, and minimise risks. You need to analyse exactly what risks are faced by the practice, how they arise, and the actions which can be taken to minimise the impact of those risks.

There is an International Standard that applies to Risk Management. This Standard—*AS/NZS ISO 31000-2009 Risk Management and Guidelines*—provides principles, framework, and a process for managing risk. It can be used by any organisation regardless of its size, activity, or sector. [18]

The Australian Compliance Institute (ACI) states: the risks faced by an organisation are varied and can be operational risk, fiduciary risk, market risk, credit and counterparty risk, legal risk and reputational risk". All of these risks can apply to healthcare practices. [19]

---

18 See International Standards: www.iso.org/iso/home/standards/iso31000. htm.
19 See the Australian Compliance Institute: www.productsafety.gov.au.

Risk could be described as the possibility that something adverse may happen to impact on the practice. Risk and its consequences on the practice are the reason practice managers need to be able to identify different types of risks and implement risk management procedures.

To assist you in identifying the sources of risk and the ways these risks may be contained, we have classified risk in four different ways:

1. Operational risks

Operational risks include working with patients, welcoming patients, collecting information from patients, and dealing with technology in consulting processes. Various problems may arise from these activities. For example, patients may feel affronted by what is said or the way in which their personal information is collected or the environment of the practice may endanger or injure patients. Many of these risks have the potential to happen on a daily basis.

2. External risks

External risks have the potential to directly impact on the practice. For example, a decision by a local council or state/federal government that changes the regulations that relate to healthcare practices has a direct impact on the practice. These risks are outside the control of the practice, but may be seen as "threats" to future prosperity.

3. Financial risks

Financial risks are a common concern for practices, given that the foremost aim of a practice is to be financially viable. For example, practice expenses and operating costs may exceed income, leading to cash problems or even financial failure. Difficulties or failure to collect fees from patients can also lead to the risk of liquidity problems. These are real concerns for practice owners which emphasises our previous issue about the need for constant and effective financial planning.

4. Legal risks

Legal risks are those covered by legislation that governs the operation of healthcare practices. This legislation can relate to contracts with suppliers, employment contracts with practice staff, general commercialisation arrangements, workers' compensation, safety legislation, professional indemnity, and professional negligence or malpractice.

Risk management begins by identifying the potential areas of risk in the practice such as:

- staff
- practice operations
- practice services
- environment and infrastructure
- external and community areas
- finance
- legal areas.

Another area to examine is past practice history. Ask yourself the following questions:

- What is the culture of the practice in relation to risk management?
- To what extent have risks arisen as a result of accidents by staff dealing with patients?
- To what extent have risks arisen as a result of staff working with external advisors or a Board of Advice?
- To what extent have risks risen as a result of the infrastructure or environment of your practice?
- What risks have arisen as a result of financial mismanagement such as failure to manage loans or failure to collect funds from debtors?

The majority of risks faced by healthcare practices are those associated with the failure of staff and patients to follow rules and regulations. Here are some examples of potential risk issues:

- breaches of confidentiality
- unauthorised activities such as disclosure of patient details
- occupational health and safety matters
- unethical behaviour towards fellow staff, patients, suppliers or other people associated with the practice.

The solution to these potential risks lies in having effective operating systems, documented procedures set out in a practice manual, appropriate education and training, and professionals providing leadership and setting an example. In order to minimise risks, your practice should have:

- a code of conduct which is to be implemented and acted upon
- a training manual which covers activities associated with potential risks
- detailed induction procedures and training programs for new staff and updated programs for continuing staff
- clear statements of staff responsibilities and authorities which are regularly reviewed
- appropriate insurance to cover all personnel associated with the practice.

In summary, risk management is an important area in terms of compliance and is one to be taken seriously.

Compliance requirements: insurance

For healthcare practices, insurance can be divided into five groups:

1. Property insurance

2. Professional indemnity insurance
3. Workers compensation insurance
4. Directors and officers insurance
5. Income protection insurance.

Property insurance

Property insurance can be divided into:

- Building insurance: if your practice is to own its own building this would be essential.
- Contents insurance: this would cover furniture, fittings, and equipment.

For both buildings and contents insurance, make sure you obtain the product disclosure statement from your insurance company to make ensure that any special conditions that relate to your practice are incorporated in the insurance policy.

Professional indemnity insurance

Staff may need to be covered with professional indemnity insurance which is designed to protect the individual from costs associated with legal actions arising due to advice given or treatment provided. Professional indemnity insurance is essential for all healthcare practices. The policy is designed to cover a healthcare professional for civil claims arising from the practice and legal and related costs associated with inquests, disciplinary procedures, enquiries, workplace disputes and/ or other claims associated with the practice. Various medical defence organisations can assist you to determine the appropriate level of cover.

Workers compensation insurance

Workers compensation insurance provides compensation benefits for workers who sustain injury or illness during the course of their employment. This form of insurance is compulsory. Workers compensation legislation in Australia aims to provide monetary and other compensation for workers injured at work or suffering an illness arising from work. Each state or territory and the Commonwealth have separate workers compensation legislation schemes.

Directors and officers liability insurance
There is also special directors and officers liability insurance which may be relevant depending on the business structure of the practice.

Income protection insurance
Finally, income protection insurance protects a person if they are unable to work due to illness or to injury of some kind. Each policy has particular requirements including waiting period duration, tax deductibility of premiums, regularity of payments and period of cover. Income protection is different from workers compensation insurance.

No discussion has been presented here on life insurance policies or disability insurance policies. Details on these types of insurance are available from insurance companies and should be a consideration as part of operating as a self-employed professional.

Insurance is necessary to protect practice operations, people, and infrastructure (including buildings, vehicles, and equipment). In terms of protecting yourself, the practice, staff, and reducing the risk of exposure to liabilities insurance of various types are essential: professional indemnity insurance, third party insurance, building and equipment insurance, and other forms of insurance is compulsory.

Insurance issues relevant to practice operations may include:
- public liability
- theft, burglary, or damage to property
- insurance covering records maintenance and protection
- insurance to cover loss of profit or performance as a result of damage to the practice
- losses or problems associated with medical equipment failure
- losses or problems associated with technical systems failure

- cash kept on the premises or in transit
- goods kept on the premises or in transit.

Insurance issues relevant to individual staff members may include:
- personal liability
- professional indemnity insurance
- income protection insurance
- superannuation
- disability income insurance
- insurance linked to sickness or injury.

Infrastructure issues relevant to infrastructure may include:
- insurance of buildings for damage
- insurance of buildings for acts of god (fire, water, or earthquakes)
- building contents (furniture, fittings and equipment)
- specialised and specified equipment
- damage to landscaping or external areas of the practice
- special cover for glass (internal and external), mirrors, windows, and signs
- personal effects of employees and patients
- vehicles used for practice operations.

Compliance requirements: patient services

Services and procedures offered to a patient may include:
- medical procedures
- referral of patients to another healthcare unit provider for medical procedures and/or testing
- team care for a patient involving communication from the initial registration to the follow-up communication after the consultation

- patient education and training
- patient consent for procedures within the practice
- secure and confidential maintenance of patient records
- privacy and confidentiality for patients at all times, including in the reception area and patient lounge
- management of infection control.

Any healthcare services and procedures offered to patients in a practice has compliance requirements associated with it. It is your responsibility to find out what these requirements are and how to meet them.

Each area of the practice has compliance obligations and these may be different for the service being offered. For example:

- professionals, practice nurses, technicians, or administrative staff will have different types of compliance requirements
- the location of where these services are provided is relevant to compliance. Services or procedures offered by the practice may be performed on-site or at a number of different sites: services offered in a practice, in a hospital, at a multi-site healthcare unit, or allied healthcare service unit will have different types of compliance requirements.

Compliance requirements: communicating with patients

Compliance issues associated with patient services relate to the collection of information and record keeping, patient consent for procedures, informed financial consent, patient billing, and Medicare compliance. Skilled communication is a critical area in terms of patient contact and compliance and can be complex due to the fact that the methods of communication to patients and the effectiveness of those methods may vary depending on the staff member. What is a suitable method of communication in one situation may not be suitable in another situation.

Staff need to be carefully trained to ensure that they use the most appropriate form of communication with a patient, taking into consideration the personal and medical factors of a patient that may impact on their ability to understand or comprehend certain messages.

As a practice owner you should keep in mind the following issues in relation to communicating with patients:

- those delivering the message (staff or professionals) are individuals with particular characteristics and how they deliver a message may impact on the success of the communication processes
- those that receive a message (the patient) are individuals with particular characteristics and how they receive a message may impact on the success of the communication process
- those that receive a message and react to it are effected by their attitude to the sender, their attitude to the message content, and their attitude to the environment in which the message was delivered (usually at the practice)
- staff that are optimistic and enthusiastic in their attitude tend to be good and effective communicators
- staff that are pessimistic and negative in their attitude tend to be poor communicators.

Communicating with patients is a complex process involving the conveying of messages that can sometimes be complicated and emotional as they relate to a patient's health and wellbeing. This communication process requires skilled staff who understand the needs of the practice's patients. Communication is an area in which compliance requirements are essential and must be taken seriously.

Compliance requirements: patient complaints

The Australian Standard on Customer Satisfaction—Guidelines for Complaints Handling in Organisations (ISO 10002-2006)[20]—is particularly important in healthcare practices. By having systems in place to manage any patient complaints you demonstrate your commitment to this regulatory requirement. This Standard has guidelines that you can adapt to develop your own specific complaints-handling program. The Australian Prudential Regulatory Authority (APRA) is responsible for managing this legislation.[21]

The following is an excerpt from the AS ISO 10002-2006:[22]

International Standard addresses the following aspects of complaints-handling:

- *enhancing customer satisfaction by creating a customer-focussed environment that is open to feedback (including complaints), resolving any complaints received, and enhancing the organization's ability to improve its product and customer service;*
- *top management involvement and commitment through adequate acquisition and deployment of resources, including personnel training;*
- *recognizing and addressing the needs and expectations of complainants;*
- *providing complainants with an open, effective and easy-to-use complaints process;*

---

20 See Australian Prudential Regulation Authority: www.apra.gov.au
21 See above n 19.
22 See *Customer Satisfaction—Guidelines for Complaints Handling in Organisations*: http://infostore.saiglobal.com/store/details. aspx?ProductID=341668

- *analysing and evaluating complaints in order to improve the product and customer service quality;*
- *auditing of the complaints-handling process;*
- *reviewing the effectiveness and efficiency of the complaints-handling process.*

The information obtained through the complaints-handling process can lead to improvements in products and processes and, where the complaints are properly handled, can improve the reputation of the organisation, regardless of size, location, and sector. In a global marketplace, the value of an International Standard becomes more evident since it provides confidence in the consistent treatment of complaints. An effective and efficient complaints-handling process reflects the needs of both the organisations supplying products and services and those who are the recipients of those products and services.

The handling of complaints through a process as described in this International Standard can enhance customer satisfaction. Encouraging customer feedback, including complaints if customers are not satisfied, can offer opportunities to maintain or enhance customer loyalty and approval and improve domestic and international competitiveness. When this Standard is applied to patient complaints it is essential that compliance with the *Privacy Act 1998* (Cth) and patient confidentiality are maintained.

We have identified four issues that are significant when dealing with patient complaints:

What is the nature of the complaint?

Consider the significance of the complaint from the perspective of your practice and how this complaint has the potential to impact on your professional reputation and the practice's reputation.

Why did the complaint arise?

Consider the factors that led to the complaint.

How should the complaint be dealt with by the practice?

Do you have a particular person who is responsible for handling patient complaints? Always notify and seek advice from your indemnity insurer. Consider whether there have been any complaints made by a patient before and how it was handled at that time.

How could this complaint have been avoided?

Consider what steps should be taken to avoid complaints of this nature arising in the future. It is important that complaints be taken seriously, investigated seriously, and dealt with in an effective manner. Any complaint made should be as a learning process for the practice.

Compliance requirements: information technology

It is an unavoidable reality that healthcare practices need to incorporate the latest in information technology in all operating systems to manage and control the practice. However, incorporating information technology has compliance implications such as: regulatory restrictions, licensing and registration requirements, and legislative requirements and restrictions. Any professional establishing a practice or joining a practice must be aware of the implications of using technology. Sources of compliance requirements include professional organisations, state, federal and local government legislation, and industry specifications.[23]

---

23 For a list of information on compliance requirements, please see the Reading List at the end of this book.

The major issues associated with compliance requirements for information technology include:

- confidentiality and security of electronic communications between professionals, staff, and patients
- the need for adequate back-up and security for records to ensure that records are protected and are readily available to the relevant staff
- managing any web-based content and websites to ensure that the practice is publicised on the internet and that this service provides appropriate information for current and potential patients
- ensuring security of online billing arrangements for patients, as well as health funds, Workcover, and Medicare
- ensuring security of online communication with for patients (this may be via a blog, a forum, or a chat room)
- ensuring adequate virus and firewall protection for all software
- regular upgrades of software
- training of personnel on the use of software programs
- preparing, drafting, and implementing practice plans for the development, maintenance, and upgrading of information technology services.

Information technology is an essential component of a successful practice and it is vital that the practice be aware of the compliance requirements associated with this.

Compliance requirements: governance

Governance refers to the overall management approach to the control of the practice and incorporates all of the compliance issues discussed in this chapter. Governance is designed to ensure that the information reaching those in charge of a practice is accurate, timely, and appropriate. These control mechanisms are to ensure that the strategies, directions, and instructions from management are carried out systematically and effectively.

Governance also relates to the following aspects of the practice:

- the culture of the practice—its mission, vision, and values—and how this culture becomes part of the practice operations
- the internal operations of the practice: the management of records, management of meetings, records from meetings, actions arising from meetings.

Governance implies that those associated with a practice are notified of any changes to the business arrangements, organisation, and structures. This again raises the issue of the quality of communication between your staff and patients. The practice should have policies and procedures in place to facilitate the effective communication of governance issues. There should also be a requirement that any changes relating to the practice and its governance are communicated to all those associated with the practice such as patients, external advisors, members of a Board of Advice, consultants, and professional organisations.

Compliance requirements: compliance management programs

In order to meet the many compliance requirements that apply to a practice—whether it be from legislation, licences, regulations, professional associations, or regulatory bodies—healthcare practices need to have structured management programs in place to ensure the actions related to compliance requirements are implemented. This program needs to involve all personnel, both internal and external.

We suggest that a compliance management program includes:

- The preparation and maintenance of a compliance register which documents key legislative and regulatory requirements for the practice. The content of the register will vary depending on the structure and organisation of the practice, practice type, practice personnel, the risk management strategies implemented into the practice, patient services offered, and information technology requirements.
- A breach register, recording mistakes, errors, omissions or complaints relating to compliance requirements. The register should include the nature of these errors, the date the breach was made, how the breach was identified, and details of any investigations undertaken and actions to rectify the breach.
- Action plans and strategies to rectify problems associated with compliance requirements for the practice and its personnel.

A compliance management program needs to be regularly reviewed. You need to constantly review and reconsider the goals and objectives of the program, the roles and responsibilities of personnel in the program, and how the program is conveyed to staff and implemented in the practice's operating systems. The aim of the program is to ensure that compliance requirements are met. We suggest that the practice compiles a team to be responsible for compliance requirements.

Compliance register

The compliance register is a substantial document and it is crucial that is recorded and stored securely and updated regularly. The compliance register should include details of compliance requirements from such sources as:

- the Australian Taxation Office
- business registration and licences requirements from government departments, professional organisations, and

business organisations; for example, the registration of a business name and licences to practice in that location
- registration associated with medical or healthcare procedures
- licences, maintenance, and agreements associated with use of specialised equipment
- Medicare
- health insurance funds whether government-based or private
- legislative requirements such as the *Corporations Act 2001* (Cth), the various *Taxation Administration Acts*, the *Privacy Act 1988* (Cth), the *Electronic Transactions Act 1999* (Cth), the various Consumer Credit Codes, and the *Fair Work Act 2009* (Cth)
- records and licences associated with professionals operating at the practice
- workplace health and safety requirements
- requirements relating to infection control and waste management
- all types of insurances associated with the practice
- record management and security
- privacy and confidentiality of patient information.

Breach register

A breach register is a vital component of ensuring that the practice meets its compliance requirements. This register allows the practice to closely monitor the way in which personnel are implementing various compliance requirements and ensures that breaches are monitored and addressed. The register must maintain details of each breach of compliance requirements: the date of the breach, who was responsible for the breach, where the breach occurred, how the breach was identified, relevant legislation or standards breached, details of the investigations undertaken, and action taken to correct the breach.

Breaches may arise in any type of healthcare practice and can be associated with personnel matters (for professionals or employed staff), risk assessment, patient services, use of information technology, and governance issues. It is vital that breaches are discussed openly with all staff to ensure that everyone in your practice recognises the importance of compliance management.

The responsibility for compliance matters in any new practice lies with the professional establishing this practice. It is the task of this professional to foster a positive culture of compliance and develop compliance-related policies. In specific terms, these professionals should do the following:

- promote a culture of compliance management amongst all personnel: full-time and part-time personnel must be involved as it is essential that every person in the practice understands the impact of compliance requirements on practice management and operations
- manage compliance in all forms through having a compliance management plan
- maintain the practice compliance register and breach register to ensure that any breaches are identified and corrected without delay
- ensure that all personnel are aware of the procedures to be followed with a compliance breach and what information has to be recorded in the breach register
- ensure that all personnel are trained in compliance matters, are aware of the sources of compliance requirements, and understand the implications of these requirements
- ensure all job descriptions include details associated with issues of compliance.

Compliance management programs need to be subject to regular reviews that take into consideration new and amended legislation, changes in any codes of conduct, and changes to standards announced and required by professional bodies or government departments—all of which may impact on compliance requirements .

Practice action for compliance breaches

Record keeping is one of the most important compliance requirements for any business. This includes recording any compliance breaches and the follow-up to such breaches. These can be recorded in the practice's compliance breach register.

As mentioned above, this register should include the complete details of:

- date of the breach
- details of the compliance breach: what, when, who was involved
- the actions to remedy the beach
- a timeframe for the actions
- a check to see the actions have been implemented.

Checklist: Compliance requirements

Question	Answer
Do staff within the practice recognise the importance of compliance requirements on practice organisation and operations?	
What specific compliance requirements are appropriate for your practice? Are you meeting all these compliance requirements?	
What sources of compliance apply to employment of personnel within your practice? Are you meeting all these compliance requirements?	
Are there specific areas of risk faced by your practice which attract compliance requirements? Are you meeting all these compliance requirements?	

Question	Answer
What specific compliance requirements apply to various insurance types for your practice? Are you meeting all these compliance requirements?	
What specific aspects of patient services attract compliance requirements and what are the compliance requirements? Are you meeting all these compliance requirements?	
What specific areas of information technology attract compliance requirements? Are you meeting all these compliance requirements?	
How will the practice organise a compliance register and who will be responsible for the register?	
How will actions within the practice be organised to meet breaches of compliance requirements and what person or team will be responsible for implementing that action?	

Chapter 10: Networking and Promotion for Practice Development

Why was this chapter written?

Networking is a process of bringing people or organisations together for the benefit of the practice. Healthcare practices rely on contact with many individuals and organisations for success; it should be self-evident as to why networking is important. Networking allows you to exchange ideas, gain knowledge from the experience of others, and bond staff to your practice. It could be argued that networking begins by bringing together the staff within the practice—breaking down the traditional barriers between professionals and non-professionals for the immediate benefit of the practice.

Promotion involves the development of the practice: growth through practice activity and patient numbers (and fees) which leads to growth in staff. There are obvious connections between networking success and promotion success and practice development. This chapter examines the various aspects of networking and promotion in practice development.

The 12 subsections of this chapter include:
1. Why was this chapter written?
2. What networking means to the practice
3. Advantages and benefits of networking

4. Networking methods
5. Networking outcomes
6. Practice development: the basics
7. Practice development: promotion
8. Practice development: continuing professional development
9. Practice development: teamwork
10. Practice development: patient needs
11. Monitoring development
12. Checklist: Networking and promotion.

What networking means to the practice

Networking is part of any successful management strategy. The process is essential to allow staff not only manage their normal daily activities but have the opportunity and enthusiasm to evaluate new ideas, systems, approaches to training, image building actions, strategies, control systems, and IT developments. In order to do this, contacts within other individuals and organisations in the healthcare industry are desirable. Networking becomes a source of knowledge for staff within your practice. This knowledge may come from individuals as advisors, professionals, and mentors, and/or organisations such as suppliers, professional groups, community groups, and government organisations.

Networking leads to progress in the management of the practice in general. For example, the benefits from networking may include increasing the number of referrals, improving practice management techniques, gaining connections or information that may be of direct benefit to the practice, providing information which may be critical for practice development, and obtaining information on government support systems. If, for example, a strategy for the practice is development through patient growth, then community networks become critical. If, on the other hand, you hope to increase efficiency, then a network of advisors or professionals in that area would take priority. Therefore, networking is not an optional extra but is a management exercise that is essential to achieve the objectives, targets, and outcomes of the practice.

Advantages and benefits of networking

An important reason why networking is a vital part of any practice's management plan are the outcomes which have the potential to change the attitudes of patients, advisors, suppliers, staff, and other stakeholders in the practice. Rather than viewing the practice as a "place to go for healthcare" only, networking creates permanent linkages, strong connections, identification with the practice, and leads to a change in attitudes by all associated with the practice.

Networking means meeting with patients, advisors, or suppliers on an informal basis outside the practice environment. It leads to continuing staff development, improved staff involvement with, and commitment to, the practice. Networking with patients and other stakeholders allows practice staff to provide information about the services available at the practice and any changes that have been incorporated into the practice.

Anecdotal evidence as well as patient survey results suggests that a majority of patients and advisors to the practice are not aware of the range of services available from healthcare practices.

Networking leads to the following five benefits:

1. Bonding patients with the practice: Staff, suppliers, and stakeholders in general are connected and bonded to the practice.
2. Problem-solving within the practice: An increase in connections leads to an increase in contacts to assist

with increases in efficiency, improvements in systems, and practice promotion of quality healthcare.

3. Provide strategic practice directions: Networking with others allows you to gain ideas and contacts that can help you establish your own point of difference, assist in practice promotion, consider practice expansion, and lead to the recruitment of new healthcare professionals.

4. Improves knowledge creation: An increase in connections through networking improves knowledge of treatment methods, technology, data, and keeps you updated with developments in the healthcare industry that might affect the practice.

5. Creates mentors: Networking allows for contact with professionals with experience who can assist in improving efficiency in the practice as well as give advice and support.

Of the above five, the two benefits that are most important for healthcare practices are assistance in providing strategic practice direction and the creation of mentors.

Strategic practice direction

Few healthcare practices have prepared formal plans of any substance in relation to the future direction of the practice. This is an area of practice management which needs to be addressed. We suggest that practice managers should place a focus on networking and its role in creating an awareness of practice strategies and gaining feedback from those involved in the practice network on alternative strategies.

Mentors

Mentors are individuals with experience and expertise in the healthcare industry. Often they are peers and it may be appropriate that internal networking with staff and external networking with patients and practice stakeholders takes place. A mentoring process is one whereby support is received in one form or another to enhance the skills or improve emotional or social adjustment and balance. This process may lead to the formation of a Board of Advice. In brief, networking leads to the strengthening and development of your practice.

Networking methods

We have previously mentioned the notion of internal and external networking. Internal networking involves staff, patients, clients, and other professionals and the methods include informal meetings, discussions, and electronic communication and online contact.

External networking involves patients, referrers, professional associations, interest groups, business contacts, stakeholders, academics, advisors, community members, governments, and healthcare institutions such as hospitals. Through a combination of internal and external networking methods, a body of experienced and professional contacts can be connected to your practice for the benefit of its future development.

There is also the use of social media to increase the practice's networking strategies: Facebook, Twitter, LinkedIn, and a strong electronic presence through the use of a practice website and email contact are vital and need to be implemented in every practice's networking plan.

Networking outcomes

We have already discussed the benefits and advantages of the networking process in this chapter. Specifically, we can identify eight outcomes from networking for your practice:

- Networking builds on the ability of the practice to meet the needs of patients and links patients to your practice in the future. Networking can strengthen the links between patients and the practice.
- Networking identifies the practice as a leader in the community and as a practice which is efficient and effective and incorporates the latest technology in its operations.
- Networking assists in the growth of patient numbers. Financial stability is a result of growth in patients, economies of scale, and efficiency. Having a financially stable practice strengthens the practice in the marketplace.
- Networking contributes to long-term sustainability and the strategic direction of your practice. Internal and external networks mean that the practice has a sound management system with provision for succession at all levels of management.
- Networking leads to an accumulation of skills and knowledge for the improvement of performance of staff and professionals. This enhances the practice's reputation.
- Networking assists communication. Internal communication systems build on practice strengths and linkages between staff and professionals.
- Networking leads to staff being involved in the delivery of quality healthcare as a team.
- Networking helps to establish a Board of Advice which becomes part of your networking process and strengthens the practice.

As a result of these outcomes, we conclude that networking has a multitude of benefits including the attraction of new patients, a growth in fees, and the continuity of growth. The remainder of this chapter deals with questions of development and practice promotion.

Practice development: the basics

Practice development is an ongoing planning activity with the objective of creating a knowledge base for the practice and introducing the changes necessary to ensure the highest quality of healthcare services to patients. Practice development is a process which focuses on practice resources.

Healthcare practices exist to provide high-quality services for patients. How these services are delivered and what is involved will change over time with new discoveries, new approaches to healthcare delivery, the increasing impact of technology, and the inevitable changes in the healthcare needs of a community. This means that you need to monitor patient requirements and have a solid financial base so that new concepts, new technologies, and new approaches to healthcare can be learnt and implemented within your healthcare practice without cost being a constraint.

In order to have the financial stability to implement new concepts and continue to develop, growth in your practice is essential. This implies that declining practice activities or maintaining the status quo is unacceptable and is unlikely to allow the practice to develop and meet the demands of change in the marketplace. Practice development involves additional costs and therefore growth is necessary to meet these costs.

Growth should be an outcome of practice development for many reasons:

- Growth may be necessary to ensure the practice remains financially viable to fund training, facilities, equipment, and other expenses associated with change.
- An increase in a range of services required by patients may require the appointment of additional staff, which automatically leads to practice growth. For example, a multi-disciplinary healthcare practice may appoint

physiotherapists, dentists, podiatrists, and dieticians to the practice.

- Growth is necessary to ensure that the practice is financially capable of meeting higher costs and increases in competition, even from the government sector. Healthcare is a politically-sensitive area and decisions by government may have an immediate and dramatic impact on the practice's financial resources.
- It is likely that the practice will specialise—requiring additional training, hiring of additional staff, and acquiring specialist facilities. Again, funds are necessary for this growth to be achieved.
- Incorporation of technologies is an outcome of growth and technology is expensive but necessary for the quality of treatment for patients.
- Practice development is part of the daily activities in a practice in the same way professional development is accepted as an ongoing activity of medical and specialist staff within your practice.

Practice development will not be achieved unless you and your staff have planned for your practice: documented the practice vision, drafted a mission statement, and written a clear statement of future objectives. This process involves examining past performance and identifying strengths and building on these strengths. It also means being frank about practice weaknesses and taking action to eliminate or reduce those weaknesses. The focus should be on locating the opportunities brought about as a result of practice development and building on those opportunities.

This suggests that practice development involves some quantitative objectives which focus on:

- the number of patients as a future objective
- the level of fees to be produced as a result of practice services

- the number of healthcare professionals and support staff to meet patient needs
- the conversion of this in terms of consulting hours, days of operation, and target number of patients per professional.

These points can be expanded into financial objectives: fees, expenses, profits, and returns on practice investment.

Practice development: promotion

Practice promotion and development involves a focus on staff: clinical staff, non-clinical staff, and teams. Practice development is only possible with the development of staff. A starting point could be non-clinical staff. Consider the following possibilities for development for non-clinical staff:

- upgrade competencies of all staff to allow multi-skilling within your practice
- ensure adequate delegation of activities and tasks so that staff have an active role in decision-making across all areas of the practice
- plan in-house and external training programs to fill any competency gaps
- review the needs of the proposed practice and identify those staff to be trained. The need for training will vary depending upon whether the emphasis is on people skills, system skills, financial management skills, or another area
- ensure you upgrade communications within the practice so that all staff are informed of the practice's vision, direction, objectives, and performance
- encourage team efforts
- encourage staff to measure their own performance against personal targets and objectives

- create a strong, loyal, dedicated staff team with networking within the practice and social activities outside practice hours
- encourage an atmosphere within the practice whereby staff come up with development ideas and are given opportunities to realise those ideas
- link performance to rewards to encourage staff. Rewards can include time off, additional recreation time, or variation in employment conditions.

Marketing and promotion is important for clinical and non-clinical staff development. The most important component of marketing is internal marketing. It can be said that internal marketing is a key to practice development since it recognises that staff impact on patients and others associated with the practice. The attitudes of staff are critical in terms of internal marketing. If staff are part of the practice vision, part of the future direction of the practice, and are confident in where the practice is going then this confidence will be implied in their dealings with patients.

As staff answer telephones, generate letters, and discuss matters face-to-face with patients an image of the practice is being developed and transmitted to patients. In this way, the practice is being "marketed" through your staff.

Practice development: continuing professional development

It is taken for granted that clinical staff are actively involved in their own professional development which impacts on practice development. As a member of a professional college or association—for example, Royal Australian College of General Practitioners, Royal Australasian College of Surgeons,

Australian Physiotherapy Association, Australian Practice Nurses Association—practitioners and staff are required to undertake a certain amount of regular professional development.

Continuing professional development requirements can vary depending on the particular college or association. Sometimes these requirements are spread over a two or three year period and can include conference attendance, online studies, practice research, professional journals.

Practice development: teamwork

A challenge for clinical staff is to recognise the importance of non-clinical staff in practice development and the progress and promotion of the practice. If this is recognised, then non-clinical staff should be given every encouragement to use their skills and knowledge to assist in the promotion of the practice. The Australian Association of Practice Managers has the Certified Practice Manager and Fellowship program that also includes continuing professional development. Such programs mean practices continue to keep up-to-date with changes and new ideas.

A challenge facing clinical staff is their willingness to be directed by practice managers (assuming a practice manager is appointed in the practice) on matters concerning management, staff, delegation, and the involvement of a Board of Advice. This challenge can often be overcome by recognising that all areas of the practice need to be managed and this is part of the role of the practice manager. This issue is in line with the notion that clinical staff should be spending as much time as possible (ideally 100 percent) dedicated to patients and patient care.

The involvement of clinical and non-clinical staff raises the questions of teamwork within the practice and the role of teams in practice development. Teamwork involves multi-skilling and an attitude of positive cooperation and coordination amongst all staff members. This in itself assists in the development and promotion of the practice through a positive image in the eyes of patients.

Associated with teamwork is the expectation that an environment is created in the practice that emphasises the importance of all staff—both clinical and non-clinical—in patient care. This needs to be created and lead by clinical staff, emphasising the importance of the attitudes of non-clinical staff involved with reception and administrative aspects of the practice. The leadership here needs to come from the professionals who own and/or run the practice.

Practice development: patient needs

A part of practice development involves meeting the needs of patients and ensuring that patients retain their links with the practice. In other words, staff should do all in their power to make the practice more valuable to patients. If patients are connected to the practice and see that connection strengthening over time, the result is a stable and growing patient base—satisfied patients will undoubtedly refer others to the practice, leading to patient growth.

The emphasis here is placed on the notion of "value adding" from the point of view of patients. How can value adding be achieved? What strategies can the practice manager and other support staff adopt to add value for patients? How can these strategies be planned and implemented?

The answers to these questions lie with practice staff—their attitudes, capabilities, previous experience, communication skills, and ability to form quality relationships with other staff and with patients. Practice development results in the practice being regarded as high value to patients when the following takes place:

- Staff are hired, nurtured, and trained and have high levels of skills and competencies and positive attitudes towards patients and their linkages with the practice.
- The practice is innovative in handling all communications with patients—in consultations, treatments, and post-consultation—creating an image which encourages patients to maintain links to the practice.
- Staff are actively involved in the healthcare industry: they are aware of the developments in the marketplace and learn from these developments and apply the knowledge gained for benefits of patients. In this way, staff are more informed of patient needs.

The patient survey

In summary, practice development means recognising patient needs. Therefore, the practice and all staff need to know their patients. In order to know more about the patients at your practice, consider conducting a patient survey. A survey may include some of the following questions in order to identify the extent of the connection between the practice and patients:

- Are patients aware of all the different services offered by your practice?
- Are all staff in the practice accessible to patients by phone, online, email or face-to-face contact?
- Are there services that patients and their families require that the practice presently does not offer?
- When patients visit the practice, do they get an impression that their thoughts and opinions are listened to by staff?
- Do the staff relate to the patient and their needs?

Common and specific needs of patients

We now turn to the common needs of patients and the specific needs of patients and the implications of these for the practice.

Common needs of patients include quality healthcare, sympathy, support, advice, technical assistance where treatment is necessary, and general considerations of confidentiality and privacy. All patients have rights and the government— for example, Department of Health—as well as healthcare professional associations, as mentioned above, spell these out in clear terms. In the majority of cases, practices recognise, accept, and implement actions to meet these common needs.

However, there are many patients who have *specific needs* and these are not always recognised by practices. These patients can be categorised into at least ten groups:

1. Young children and babies
2. Young adults
3. Families with children
4. Single parents with dependent children
5. Parents without dependent children
6. Retirees (supported by government or self-funded)
7. Adults who may have lost a partner
8. Various ethnic groups where English is a second language spoken
9. Patients with chronic illnesses
10. Patients with special disabilities.

The above list is not exhaustive, but does identify the range of special needs that may be found within any group of patients. You need to identify whether your practice can recognise these needs and treat patients accordingly. This may require significant changes to the operating methods of the practice.

Monitoring development

We have suggested in this chapter that networking takes place, promotional activities be implemented, and all staff be involved in the development of the practice. What follows from this is the need to monitor the outcomes of practice development. Any recording or reporting of outcomes and actions is the responsibility of a non-clinical staff member, not the professional responsible for practice operations. Staff can be trained to undertake this monitoring process effectively and efficiently.

Monitoring practice development involves the following considerations:

- Details of networks: patients, professionals, internal networks among staff, external networks among potential patients
- Details of professional development programs (internal or external) completed by non-clinical staff and their reaction to those programs
- Professional development programs attended by clinical staff and their reaction to those programs
- Identification of special needs of patients and the ability of your practice to meet those special needs
- Teams established or proposed to be established within the practice and the membership of such teams
- The number of new patients admitted to the practice and basis for admission
- Outcomes of patient surveys and recommendations on actions.

Part of practice development involves the inclusion of a strategy whereby action is taken at particular points in time and monitored. A pattern can be developed which allows you to monitor and take action on a regular basis.

Checklist: Networking and promotion

Question	Answer
How do you interpret networking for your practice?	
What groups in your practice are involved in networking? Is this current arrangement successful?	
What do you see as the main advantage from networking for your practice?	
Do you see advantages and benefits from networking from the point of view of patients?	
What networking methods are currently working for your practice? What new methods do you need to adopt?	
What do you see as the most important outcome from your networking methods?	
What do you see as the main aim or objective of practice development?	

Question	Answer
For the first 12 months of any new practice, what practice development strategies do you see as being important?	
Can you identify patient needs and link these to your proposed practice development program?	
Can you nominate a staff member who will be responsible for monitoring networking, promotions and development and identify action to be taken as a result of that monitoring process?	

Chapter 11: Starting Practice: A Review

Why was this chapter written?

This chapter represents a culmination of the topics discussed in Chapters 1 to 10. The issues covered in these chapters help you to identify what is required to create a successful healthcare practice. In other words, if you:

- believe you have the qualities to establish a successful healthcare practice
- can reflect on the various options of self-employment that are available to you
- can attract new patients and convert current patients to become practice ambassadors
- identify areas of barriers to patient satisfaction
- recognise that your most important practice asset is quality staff
- implement efficient IT systems
- have reporting and planning methods of financial performance
- meet compliance requirements
- undertake networking for practice development

then you understand what is required to establish a successful practice that generates profits, creates a rewarding employment opportunity for staff, and provides an outstanding level of quality healthcare. This chapter serves as a review of the book and a conclusion of sorts.

The 12 subsections of this chapter include:

1. Why was this chapter written?
2. Key points from Chapter 1
3. Key points from Chapter 2
4. Key points from Chapter 3
5. Key points from Chapter 4
6. Key points from Chapter 5
7. Key points from Chapter 6
8. Key points from Chapter 7
9. Key points from Chapter 8
10. Key points from Chapter 9
11. Key points from Chapter 10
12. Personal recommendations.

At this point, we emphasise how important it is to have a complete understanding of the issues relating to starting a healthcare practice. Central to this is the notion of a practice image—this is the outcome of the perceptions by those connected to your practice: patients, clinicians, suppliers, referrers, government representatives, and members of the community. Image represents the attitudes of the community and the healthcare profession towards your practice.

Ideally, this image is that your practice has a sense of creativity and a willingness to be innovative and provide leadership within the community. This recognition leads to extended recognition by other professionals in the industry, by members of the community, by government representatives, and by staff within your practice.

The key group to promote your practice image are your patients. What patients experience in your practice, hear about your practice, and experience with your practice will make a positive impression. A practice with a positive image will be viewed as a leader in the profession and community, attracting high-quality staff and patients who have the highest opinion of the practice quality and become practice ambassadors.

Key points from Chapter 1: The qualities to establish a successful healthcare practice

Chapter 1 examined the qualities of individuals who wish to start a successful healthcare practice. The chapter looked at attitudes to workplace requirements, compliance, and factors that would have a positive impact on the success of the practice. Here we are interested in this question: to what extent do these factors impact on practice image?

The qualities of healthcare professionals

The image of any healthcare practice can be affected significantly by the attitudes and qualities of the individuals providing leadership in those practices. These individuals focus on caring for patients and as such are dedicated, determined, optimistic, impartial, and tend to be leaders. They are willing to listen, seek solutions to problems, and act as counsellors and advisors to their patients. These attitudes are significant factors in building practice image.

Characteristics of the self-employed professional

Self-employed professionals are decision-makers. Every key decision regarding the practice and its operations rests with the professional: the location of the practice, practice layout, systems, employing and training staff, safety and planning, and building a significant reputation in the marketplace. These tasks are demanding but the rewards are significant.

Attitudes to the workplace

The personal characteristics of professionals are directly related to workplace conditions: the ability to communicate with staff, self-confidence and self-reliance, the ability and willingness to listen, and high levels of skilled communication. The workplace of a practice involves patients—people with different requirements and concerns. Each self-employed professional becomes a leader with an ability to adjust to different patient requirements and to provide guidance to staff and those associated with their practice.

Attitudes to compliance

Every practice will face the need to comply with the regulations and requirements of various organisations including government, regulatory bodies, and professional associations. Each professional has to accept that compliance is "part of the job" and is in the interests of patients, even though it may seem that compliance applies constraints to the practice. Compliance has an impact on business structure, professionals, personnel, services, information technology, risk, and corporate governance.

Reasons not to seek self-employment

The end of Chapter 1 identified how professionals may seek self-employment for the wrong reasons, including the accumulation of wealth, seeking social status, apparent freedom on the use of time and management, the pursuit of power, and as a result of peer pressure. Entering self-employment and establishing an independent practice for any of these reasons will not enhance the image of the practice but will have the opposite effect. This content is critical for success for healthcare professionals seeking self-employment. Close attention should be paid to all these areas particularly if the objective is to build on practice image.

Key points from Chapter 2:
Self-employment options and implications

Chapter 2 examined business options and the implications for development as a self-employed professional. We identified four possible options for business structure: individual private practices, practice partnerships, associateships, and incorporated practices. We discussed the fact that corporate ownership is increasing with public and private companies buying professional practices and contracting with practitioners to provide and deliver professional services. Despite these developments, the role of the sole practitioner continues and is particularly important in the field of general healthcare practice.

To these four options we could add a further option: you remaining in salaried employment on a part-time basis and operate as a self-employed practitioner in your available time. For example, you could remain as a part-time employee of a hospital while also operating as a self-employed practitioner. All options in Chapter 2 could be varied to allow modifications in work conditions. Self-employment does not necessarily mean full-time employment as a sole practitioner; many options as a self-employed professional exist.

Importance of business structure

Governments, patients, staff, management, and businesses within the community are entitled to know what type of organisation they are dealing with when they connect with a healthcare practice. Each of the above have a particular reason for this knowledge: governments because of the need to monitor compliance requirements; patients are entitled to know the relationship between themselves and the practice and its staff; staff have a significant interest in the structure of the practice and need to know whether they are employed by an individual, a group of individuals, a company, or some alternative organisation. The structure of the business will affect who is responsible for managing the business, their responsibilities and accountabilities.

Sole practitioner

The sole practitioner is a person who may carry on the practice as a business in his or her own right as a proprietor whether in a personal name or a business name. There are advantages and disadvantages of the sole practitioner option and these must be recognised by those establishing the new enterprise.

Associates, partnership, trust, or corporation

Associates are practitioners who share premises and expenses on an agreed basis but generally retain their own fees from consultations. Associates share infrastructure but do not share the outcomes of their consultation services. Associateships have significant advantages and disadvantages and must be reviewed by those establishing a practice and those employing additional professionals.

Partnerships are a structure where several practitioners come together to establish a practice, offer services, and share management, administration, and profits. State legislation exists to govern partnerships where no specific agreement exists. There are advantages and disadvantages of this type of organisation. Legal advice is essential in establishing a partnership. The same applies to establishing trusts and a corporation or service company.

Business names and registration

Each practice normally has a business name to trade under and to identify it in the marketplace—this business name being different from any company or any name used within the healthcare industry. Business names are registered on a national basis.

Healthcare registration is essential and required by an appropriate registration board depending upon the healthcare field. As discussed in Chapter 2, registration boards—for example, AHPRA, colleges and associations, and Medicare—are responsible for healthcare operations and have regulatory roles. They are responsible for the quality of healthcare provided to the community and have a function to investigate complaints.

In addressing business names and details of healthcare registration, it is essential to obtain legal advice. Accreditation is associated with registration and ensures that practice image is maintained as accreditation is regarded as a measure of quality control representing an efficient and effective healthcare practice.

Advertising

While the newly established healthcare practice must provide information on its location, services, personnel and operations to the community, there are constraints on the amount and format of advertising that can be used. It is the responsibility of each professional to obtain details from the appropriate professional body. The Medical Board of Australia has produced guidelines for advertising in regulated health services in Australia before proceeding with any advertising campaign.[24] There are generally no restrictions to promotion and advertising within the practice through signage, notices, photographs, and the equivalent. This is to be encouraged as it has a positive impact on the image of the practice.

Key points from Chapter 3: Attracting and retaining patients

Chapter 3 focussed on attracting and retaining patients and converting patients to become practice ambassadors: patients who would actively seek to persuade others to consult with your practice. In achieving this objective, a number of key issues were discussed.

---

24 See the Medical Board of Australia: www.medicalboard.gov.au.

Impact of practice location

The location of a new healthcare practice is likely to be heavily affected by the specific interests of professionals. For example, professionals may tend to locate a new practice near their residence. In considering the establishment of a practice, it is accepted that practice location has an impact on the attraction of potential patients and on practice image. These factors must be considered when making decisions regarding location.

Role of professionals and staff

Chapter 3 emphasised the importance of individuals in building patient numbers and retaining patients. The reality is that when patients decide to leave a practice for an alternative practice, the reasons are likely to be linked to unacceptable behaviour or attitudes of staff within that practice. Chapter 3 emphasised the importance of carefully selecting staff and providing adequate training. Staff behaviour and attitudes has a significant impact on patient numbers.

Building patient numbers: reputation and image

In the initial years of a practice, reputation and image are critical in terms of building patient numbers. While some potential patients may be attracted to a practice because of its convenient location, in the longer term reputation and image is critical to building and retaining numbers.

Building patient numbers: practice services and patient follow-up

To some extent, services and follow-up are part of practice image and reputation. However, it is significant for services to be designed and launched in a way that meets the needs of potential patients. In addition, contact with patients beyond consultations by way of follow-up is significant to building image and reputation. These two aspects of practice activities are important to the long-term success of the practice.

Retaining patients as practice ambassadors

Practice ambassadors are those patients who are completely satisfied with all aspects of your practice and actively seek to encourage others to consult with your practice. There are many patients who may be "satisfied" with the practice but are not driven to actively encourage others to consult with your practice. What is to be avoided are the situations that result in negative attitudes of patients which is detrimental to building of patient numbers for your practice.

Chapter 3 commented on the importance of practice services, patient follow-up, creating your practice as a healthcare centre, internal referrals (converting patients to practice ambassadors), and setting targets for patient numbers. The content in this chapter is critical to the success of a new healthcare practice: success means attracting and retaining patients.

Key points from Chapter 4: Patient satisfaction

Chapter 4 examines issues to maximise patient satisfaction: to remove barriers faced by patients in dealing with the practice. Those wishing to establish a new healthcare practice need to recognise the potential for such barriers and take action to eliminate these barriers before they arise.

Barriers faced by patients

The barriers identified as reducing patient satisfaction from consultations include excess waiting time, problems associated with gathering patient information, problems associated with supplying patient information, the physical layout of the practice, administrative procedures, staff attitudes, and attitudes of professionals. We make the point that, in general, patients are satisfied with the advice and care they receive from clinicians. This then suggests that many of the problems are associated with other issues in the practice such as staff attitudes or procedures.

Waiting time and information

Waiting time is seen as a major problem for patients. This can be the time required to obtain a consultation, delays in completing administrative procedures, waiting time for consultation, and waiting time associated with post-consultation procedures.

Gathering information from patients and providing information to patients are also seen as major barriers. This may be in terms of a lack of information on procedures to be followed, lack of information on data required by the professional which was not advised to the patient in advance, and lack of information on aspects of consultation and procedures in the practice or in associated healthcare centres such as hospitals.

Practice layout and procedures

Practice layout is seen as a major problem for patients. Inadequate layout of the reception area can fail the requirement of confidentiality and security in terms of patient information. The practice needs to have a layout that allows for conversations between patient and staff relating to outcomes of consultations and billing issues to be confidential. Failure to have this layout will cause significant dissatisfaction amongst patients.

Use of technology

Inappropriate use of technology is seen as a major problem for patients. There are significant opportunities for technology to be applied in all matters associated with patient administration within the practice. This includes initial contact between the patient and practice, communication within the practice, communication between clinicians and patients, and communication with patients following consultation. In the majority of cases, technology is not effectively applied. Practices need to be aware of this and implement adequate use of technology to improve the image of the practice and increase patient satisfaction.

Personnel

The performance of personnel is seen as a major problem for patients. This book emphasises the importance of staff in the healthcare industry to develop a positive image for the healthcare practice. Personnel can present a significant barrier to patients if they have poor behaviour and attitudes. This may be due to a lack of planning, particularly from a clinician who fails to plan for each consultation. The solution is adequate training, monitoring, establishing standards, and maintaining those standards.

Key points from Chapter 5: The importance of staff

Chapter 5 focuses on the importance of quality staff. This chapter emphasised that although professionals are responsible for providing consulting services, the majority of contact that patients have in your practice is with staff. It follows that the attitudes, behaviour, and assistance that staff may or may not give to patients has a significant impact on practice success and practice image.

Qualities of hired staff

Initially, this chapter emphasised the entrepreneurial attitudes of staff, the need for staff to fill designated positions within your practice, and the requirement for staff who were IT literate. Employing such staff are important for building on practice quality and practice image.

Promoting leadership and building teams

Staff are expected to be leaders in all aspects of their employment, whether it be dealing with patients arriving at your practice for the first time, handling telephone calls, dealing with systems, or handling practice records. Any practice requires teams to be able to handle a range of activities and members of a team need not be full-time staff members but could be those associated with your practice on a part-time basis. Flexibility is essential in meeting needs of your practice.

Encourage management of performance

From their first day of appointment, staff should be encouraged to manage their own performance, critically evaluate their performance, and improve their performance. The professionals in charge of your practice cannot be expected to allocate endless hours to the performance measurement of staff. If staff are trained to measure their own performance and control their own performance, then practice image is significantly improved.

Bringing out the best in individuals

It is essential for professionals to possess a positive attitude with staff in order to build image and correct attitudes. Staff require assistance, guidance, training, and monitoring of their performance but if professionals take the view that they should bring out the best in their staff, then this will have a positive impact on practice image.

The importance of staff in building and maintaining a positive practice image cannot be underestimated. Those considering establishing a new healthcare practice must place significant emphasis on the careful selection of staff and the training, monitoring, and development of staff to have a positive approach to patients and your practice as a whole.

Key points from Chapter 6: Using technology effectively

Chapter 6 emphasises the importance of your practice being a "paperless" office with professionals and support staff utilising technology to provide services. The emphasis in Chapter 6 is on computer-based systems to contribute to ongoing practice image.

Patient communication, consultation records, recalls, and referrals

These issues are at the centre of practice activities and ensures your practice maintains a positive image. The importance of patient communication and records cannot be overemphasised. The same applies to patient recalls and referrals. All of these need to be undertaken effectively and efficiently for any practice to have a positive image.

Financial records and reports

The financial performance of your practice is essential for a positive image. Records must be effectively maintained and reports produced to represent financial performance of the practice. Financial performance has an impact on staff attitudes and patients will expect the practice to be financially strong.

Personnel

Quality staff are an important asset for any newly established practice. Issues such as recruitment, professional development of staff, and staff performance must be at the forefront of your practice management if your practice is to be seen as effective and efficient.

Systems and records

Details contained in records and office systems are often confidential and require protection. Specific software systems are available for this purpose. Insurance also has a role in protecting information within the practice. These are matters that need to be investigated and taken seriously by those that wish to ensure that practice image is maintained and increases over time.

Office technology

Up-to-date office technology is essential to ensure effective communication with patients, adequate and safe record keeping, and systems which work successfully with current and potential patients. Careful selection of office technology is essential for this purpose as well as for the image of your practice.

Key points from Chapter 7: Financial performance

It is so important to understand that a healthcare practice is a business and it is essential to understand what is required to make your practice viable. We discussed the value and the role of external advisors such as an accountant and a Board of Advice. Realising the value of financial reporting and how to use them in your practice helps you to know your practice and underpin many of the business decisions you make. This chapter also emphasised the link between quality of healthcare services and the financial performance of the practice.

The practice as a business

This section discusses the practice as a business with the emphasis on understanding where and how income is produced, the costs of running a practice, and the need to be able to deliver quality services while containing expenses and making a profit. We also discuss using benchmarks to understand the relationship between income, costs and profit.

Financial terms

Understanding financial terms is important and in this section, we explained financial terms as they specifically apply to a healthcare practice.

Practice viability

Practice viability is not often discussed in relation to healthcare practices but Chapter 7 makes the link between the quality, range, and growth of practice services and the control of practice expenses to ensure the viability of the practice.

Financial reports

A discussion about the value of financial reports was presented with examples of the type of reports to consider. This section also gave the opportunity to plan for the reports that might be important in your particular practice. Guiding staff to collect and report on financial matters and the role of the practice manager was discussed with the emphasis on the ability of staff to take responsibility for providing you with the financial reporting and analysis that is critical for your understanding of the complete financial sustainability of your practice and where you are in relation to your financial goals.

Board of Advice

We focussed here on the benefits of using a Board of Advice and what to expect from such a group of advisors in regards to the development of the practice, future plans and direction.

External accountant

In this section, we raised the issue of the role of an external accountant which can extend beyond simply advising on taxation matters. An external accountant can become involved in your practice from the beginning with advice on what financial systems you should establish. You might consider an accountant for taxation advice and another to provide you with wider financial advice.

Quality of service and financial performance

Quality of service and financial performance was discussed and the link made between the ability to attract patients by demonstrating the quality of services through such examples as practice accreditation, service standards, abilities of personnel and the core values of the practice.

Measuring financial performance

Here we were able to demonstrate the value of both measuring financial performance and using graphs and charts to present actual data to illustrate any variations in practice performance. Charts and graphs can be used to assist decision-making in a practice.

Practice billing

Practice billing and collection of fees due was the focus of this section. Understanding these two processes are an important part of managing an effective practice. This includes how fees are set, how they are billed, and how they are collected. Billing policies are an essential part of the financial performance.

Key points from Chapter 8: Financial planning

Chapter 8 emphasises the importance of financial planning. The chapter makes it clear that financial planning is not an optional extra; it is essential for the progress and development of the practice and the practice image. It is likely that most professionals establishing a new practice need advice from a financial planner.

Planning is not an optional extra

Preparing a financial plan is essential for the new practice; it is not an optional extra. It may be argued that establishing a new practice without a financial plan is asking for disaster in terms of sustainability and profitability. It is strongly suggested that readers discuss their financial plans with a qualified accountant.

Planning with benchmarks

Understanding expenses related to patients and expenses related to practice operations is a complex matter and needs to be understood by practitioners. A successful practice must operate at a profit and practitioners need to understand how such profits can be generated. Benchmarks represent standards of performance which can act as incentives to improve performance. Benchmarks establish what should be achieved by the practice and how the practice should develop.

Focus on patients, fees, and cash flow

Professionals establishing a new practice must understand the relationship between patients, fees, and cash flow. Cash flow is affected by the operations of the practice and is not directly linked to patient numbers. This relationship involves understanding practice overheads and setting standards for overall performance taking into consideration patients, fees, and overheads. Again, advice from a professional accountant is advisable.

Working with external specialists

We recommend seeking the advice and assistance of accountants or financial qualified consultants when establishing a new practice. Arrangements between the practice, staff, and external specialists must be understood and documented carefully so that practitioners obtain the required information in order to meet performance standards. These external specialists need to be carefully selected and assessed in order to ensure they can provide timely information for the practice which is relevant to maintaining a standard of performance.

Personnel, financial planning, and control

Throughout this chapter, we emphasise the importance of personnel on practice performance and success. The "negative" aspect of the link between personnel and performance is the fact that personnel can adversely influence performance and practice image. Most, if not all, expenses associated with performance are the result of personnel. If personnel are not carefully controlled, practice performance can be a disaster. Personnel need to be carefully trained on all aspects of practice expenses, management of practice revenue, and how their actions can influence the financial performance of the practice.

Key points from Chapter 9: Compliance and risk management

Chapter 9 examines the compliance requirements and risk management issues associated with a practice: the requirements set by governments, professional organisations, and the community. We emphasise that meeting these requirements is not optional—any breach of compliance requirements has legal implications and a negative impact on the reputation of the practice. Compliance is the outcome of the practice meeting its obligations to third parties. Compliance requirements can be stipulated in any Act, licence, regulation, decision of regulatory bodies, and professional association. The outcome of meeting the compliance requirement is that practices can demonstrate standards of good governance, ethics, and community expectations. Compliance has an impact on practice organisation and type, personnel, risk, patient services, and information technology. Hence, a management program for compliance is essential for all practices.

Recognising the impact of compliance requirements

Compliance requirements flow from various Acts at Commonwealth and state levels and include registration and licences, copyright issues, specialist equipment, and insurance requirements. Compliance has a significant impact on the employment of personnel, the methods that personnel communicate with patients, and on all aspects associated with practice management.

Compliance: practice type and personnel

The structure of the practice—whether the practice is a private practice, corporate practice, or associated with a hospital— determines compliance requirements as they relate to location, patient registration, informed consent of patients, billing requirements, and communicating the outcomes of consultations to patients. In addition, the practice is required to be compliant with registration obligations and licences associated with equipment and procedures. Personnel—both internal and external—may have an impact on compliance requirements.

Compliance requirements impact on any codes of conduct of the practice, registration required for clinical professionals, the referral of patients to the practice, and the referral of patients to other healthcare practices. Compliance requirements also apply to titles, wages and salaries, recruitment procedures, workplace operations, workplace health and safety requirements, and insurance.

Compliance: risk management and insurance

Risk is associated with the operational aspects of the healthcare practice: working with patients, registration of patients, collecting information from patients, and using technology in the consulting process. Other risks may arise outside the practice such as local government changes and changes to legislation. Some risk is associated with finance and financial planning. There are risks that apply to the employment of personnel. For example, these risks may include breaches of confidentiality, unauthorised activities such as disclosure of patient details, risks associated with occupational health and safety, and unethical behaviour.

Insurance is an issue directly associated with risk management. Practices need to implement adequate insurance to cover personnel, operations, physical assets, and professional indemnity.

Compliance: patient services and technology

Compliance requirements associated with patient services and technology are particularly important for practices. Patient services may include medical procedures, referring patients to other practices, patient education, patient consent for procedures, privacy and confidentiality issues, and the management of infection control within the practice.

Technology is important because it is part of the communication system that exists between the practice and its patients. Privacy and confidentiality are directly related to this issue. The practice is expected to ensure adequate back-up and security of records, management of web-based policies and procedures, security of online billing arrangements, regular upgrades of software and equipment, training of personnel on software and use of technology, and implementation of practice plans for developing information technology.

Management programs for compliance requirements

Healthcare practices are expected to have a structure which incorporates the review of compliance requirements including the preparation of a breach register recording errors or omissions and action taken to correct problems associated with compliance mismanagement. Completion of the register and action following review of the register should be a regular feature of practice operations.

Key points from Chapter 10: Networking and promotion for practice development

Chapter 10 examines networking and promotion for the new practice. This is an essential component of maintaining and developing a practice image. Networking is the process of bringing people or organisations together for the benefit of the practice. Promotion means expanding on what has already been developed for the practice.

Networking and promotion

Networking can include internal and external personnel. Networking may begin by bringing together personnel within the practice to break down barriers between professionals and non-professionals for the benefit of practice management and progress. Promotion can be defined as growth within practice activity through patient numbers and fees which lead to growth in personnel. Both networking and promotion are part of successful management strategies. Networking produces new ideas, new systems, new approaches to training, new image-building action, new strategies, new control systems, and new IT developments. Networking and promotion should be automatic activities of strategic management within a new practice.

Networking methods and outcomes

Networking involves bringing together staff, professionals, patients, and external advisors and could include face-to-face contact, informal meetings, discussions, and online communication. Networking may involve patients, business contacts, stakeholders, academics, advisors, and community members, as well as representatives of governments and healthcare institutions such as hospitals. The outcomes of networking include meeting the needs of patients, image-building, financial stability through growth, long-term stability, accumulation of skills and knowledge, and establishing wide-reaching connections for the practice and its staff.

Practice development and patient needs

Meeting patient needs can only result from detailed knowledge of patients through personal contact or specific practice surveys. There are common and specific needs of patients and these needs have to be recognised. This chapter identifies groups of patients ranging from young children through to retirees. Monitoring practice development in light of these details is essential for the practice image to be developed and maintained.

Monitoring programs and action

Networking and promotion programs need to be monitored to ensure action is forthcoming otherwise the exercises will be, to a large extent, a waste of time from the point of view of developing and maintaining a practice image. The monitoring and review program needs to be continuous and not something which occurs occasionally. The outcomes of monitoring and action programs should be the subject of discussions in practice team meetings.

Personal recommendations

Finally, in Chapter 11 we recommend that users of this book review the above summaries and refer to each chapter for additional details and information to obtain a clear understanding of what is required to develop and maintain a positive practice image.

The remainder of this chapter provides a list of recommendations to be used to develop and maintain practice image. Use these worksheets to decide what you believe to be the importance of each of the summaries in the 10 chapters of this book to the operation of your practice. The first set of worksheets require you to list, in order of importance, the recommendations given in each chapter. The second set of worksheets require you to note your ability or concerns to practically implement the suggestions given in each chapter. The third set of worksheets requires you to examine key areas where additional attention is required.

Personal recommendations: Chapters 1-10

Chapter 1

_____

_____

_____

_____

Chapter 2

_____

_____

_____

_____

Chapter 3

_____

_____

_____

_____

Chapter 4

_____

_____

_____

_____

Chapter 5

_____

_____

_____

_____

Chapter 6

_____

_____

_____

_____

Chapter 7

_____

_____

_____

_____

Chapter 8

_____

_____

_____

_____

Chapter 9

_____

_____

_____

_____

Chapter 10

_____

_____

_____

_____

Implementing personal recommendations

Chapter 1

_____

_____

_____

_____

Chapter 2

_____

_____

_____

_____

Chapter 3

_____

_____

_____

_____

Chapter 4

_____

_____

_____

_____

Chapter 5

_____

_____

_____

_____

Chapter 6

_____

_____

_____

_____

Chapter 7

_____

_____

_____

_____

Chapter 8

Chapter 9

Chapter 10

The need to update my knowledge

Based on my knowledge of the content and my ability to use the information in Chapters 1–10, I recommend that I pay attention to the following four areas:

Area 1:

_____

_____

_____

_____

Area 2:

_____

_____

_____

_____

Area 3:

_____

_____

_____

_____

Area 4:

_____

_____

_____

_____

Reading List

Adair, John. *100 Greatest Ideas for Amazing Creativity*. United Kingdom: Capstone, 2011

Bacal, Robert. *How to manage performance*. Sydney: McGraw-Hill Professional Education Series, 2004

Ballen, John. *Computer Basics*. London: Pearson, 2009

Brinkman, Rick and Kirchner, Rick. *Dealing with difficult people*. Sydney: McGraw-Hill Professional Education Series, 2004

Bruce, Anne. *How to motivate every employee*. Sydney: McGraw-Hill Professional Education Series, 2004

Clayton, Martin. *Brilliant team management*. United Kingdom: Pearson, 2011

Goleman, Daniel, Richard Boyatzis and Annie McKee. *The New Leaders*. London: Time Warner Paperbacks, 2002

Huszczo, Gregory. *Tools for Team Excellence*. California: Davies-Black Publishing, 2006

Kruger Wilson, Cathleen and Timothy Porter-O'Grady. *Leading the Revolution in Health Care* (Second Edition) Maryland: Aspen Publishers Inc, 1999

Lamm, Jacob et al. *Under Control: Governance Across the Enterprise.* New York: Apress, 2009

Maginn, Michael. *Making teams work.* Sydney: McGraw-Hill, 2004

McManus, Sean. *Web Design In Easy Steps Ltd.* London: in Easy steps Ltd, 2011

Meredith, Geoffrey. *21ˢᵗ Century Medical Practice Management.* Brisbane: Mereton Publishings, 2006

Murtagh, John. *John Murtagh's General Practice 5ᵗʰ ed.* Sydney: McGraw Hill, 2010

Norton, Robert. *Get a Quest!* USA: CreateSpace Independent Publishing Platform, 2014

Norton, Robert. *Treat People Like Dogs! Six Tasks for Passionate Leaders.* Montana: Wild Norton Fire, 2005

Pease, Alan and Barbara. *Body Language in the Workplace.* London: Pease International, 2011

Rispin, Craig. *How to Think Like a Futurist—Know First, Be First, Profit First.* North Ryde: The Future Trends Group, 2009

Rowntree, Derek. *Brilliant Checklists for Managers.* London: Pearson, 2011

Slater, Rus. *Getting Things Done.* United Kingdom: HarperCollins Reference, 2011

Sullivan, Colleen and Geoffrey Meredith. *Successful Practice Management*. USA: Lulu Books, 2012

Turner, Colin. Lead to Succeed: *Creating Entrepreneurial Organisations*. UK: Texere Publishing Company, 2002

Williams, Kevin. *Brilliant Business Plan: What to Know and Do to Make the Perfect Plan*. London: Penguin, 2011

Zenger, John and Joseph Folkman. *Handbook for Leaders*. Sydney: McGraw-Hill, 2004

Websites

The website references below are just some examples of information that is available on the internet. There are many other sites that will be helpful for anyone starting practice or involved in healthcare practice.

Associations
Australian Association of Practice Managers www.aapm.org.au

Australian Dental Association www.ada.org.au

Australian Medical Association www.ama.com.au

Australian Physiotherapy Association www.physiotherapy.asn.au

Government resources
Australian Bureau of Statistics www.abs.gov.au

Australian Competition and Consumer Commission www.accc.gov.au

Australian Health Practitioner Agency www.ahpra.gov.au

Australian Securities and Investments Commission www.asic. gov.au

Australian Taxation Office www.ato.gov.au

Compliance Australia www.compliance.org.au

Department of Human Services www.humanservices.gov.au

Fairwork Australia Ombudsman www.fairwork.gov.au

Health Workforce Australia www.hwa.gov.au

Medical Board of Australia www.medicalboard.gov.au.

Medicare Australia www.medicareaustralia.gov.au

Safe Work Australia www.safeworkaustralia.gov.au

Standards Australia www.standards.org.au

Medical colleges

Australasian College of Emergency Medicine www.acem.org.au

Australian and New Zealand College of Anaesthetists www. anzca.edu.au

Australian College of Rural and Remote Medicine www.acrrm. org.au

Royal Australasian College of Physicians www.racp.edu.au

Royal Australasian College of Surgeons www.surgeons.org.

Royal Australian and New Zealand College of Ophthalmologists www.ranzco.edu

Royal Australian College of General Practitioners www.racgp. org.au

The Royal College of Pathologists Australasia www.rcpa.edu.au

Accreditation

Australian General Practice Accreditation Ltd www.agpal.com.au

GPA Accreditation www.gpa.net.au

Quality in Practice www.qip.com.au

Royal Australian College of General Practitioners. *Standards for general practices* (4th edition) www.racgp.org.au/your-practice/standards

Practice tools

Australian Compliance Institute www.productsafety.gov.au

My Practice Manual www.mypracticemanual.com

Performance Measurement www.staceybarr.com

Stanford Entrepreneurial Network http://sen.stanford.edu

Wikipedia www.wikipedia.org

Journals

Australian Association of Practice Managers. *The Practice Manager*. Melbourne: www.aapm.org.au

Australian Medical Association Journal

Australian Medical Association State Journals e.g. *Doctor Q, The NSW Doctor*

Pulse Magazine. *Pulse +IT*. Melbourne: Pulse+It Magazine Pty Ltd

Other resources

Australian Association of Practice Managers www.aapm.org.au

Avant Mutual Group, *Getting Started in Private Practice* via www.avant.org.au

Royal Australian College of General Practitioners. *Discussion Paper: A quality general practice of the future* via www.racgp.org.au

UNE Partnerships *Professional Practice Management Development Program* via www.unep.edu.au

Medical Defence Organisations

Avant Mutual Group www.avant.org.au

MDA National www.mdanational.com.au

Medical Indemnity Protection Society www.mips.com.au

Medical Insurance Group Australia www.miga.com.au

Author Biographies

Colleen Sullivan
OAM, B.A., FAAPM, Dip Prac Man.

Colleen Sullivan has over 25 years experience in practice management. She has a strong commitment to healthcare practice management and the role of the practice manager. For most of her career, Colleen has been actively involved with the Australian Association of Practice Managers (AAPM) and held positions of State and National Presidents. She is a Fellow and Life Member of the Association.

She is a presenter and assessor for UNE Partnerships Professional Practice Management Program.

Colleen has been an invited presenter at local, national, and international healthcare conferences for AAPM, the Royal Australia College of General Practitioners, the Australian Medical Association, Specialist Medical Colleges, the Australian Dental Association, and other Allied Health Associations.

Colleen has a background in nursing and is a graduate of University of Queensland. Colleen and Professor Meredith have worked collaboratively on other practice management projects.

In 2014, Colleen was awarded the Medal of the Order of Australia for her services to medical administration in the Queen's Birthday Honours 2014.

Geoffrey Meredith
AM, PhD, MAAPM(Hon)

Emeritus Professor Geoffrey Meredith has advised, planned, and presented executive development programs for clinicians and practice managers in private practice since the 1970s. Many presentations have been in sessions organised by professional healthcare organisations.

His intense interest is in assisting healthcare practices organise resources to ensure that quality services for patients provide value and satisfaction from each consultation with a contribution to this satisfaction from not only clinicians but also from practice support staff and practice systems.

He is the author of more than 20 books on management including *21ˢᵗ Century Medical Practice Management* and articles on healthcare management in professional journals.

A graduate of the University of Queensland and also an honorary member of the Australian Association of Practice Managers, he has presented programs on private practice management in New Zealand, Canada, and Asia.

www.ingramcontent.com/pod-product-compliance
Lightning Source LLC
Chambersburg PA
CBHW072100020426
42334CB00017B/1574